Quick **BIBLE** Quizzes

Prove Your **BIBLE KNOWLEDGE** in 300 Categories

Sara Stoker

© 2023 by Barbour Publishing, Inc.

ISBN 978-1-63609-603-2

All rights reserved. No part of this publication may be reproduced or transmitted for commercial purposes, except for brief quotations in printed reviews, without written permission of the publisher. Reproduced text may not be used on the World Wide Web.

Churches and other noncommercial interests may reproduce portions of this book without the express written permission of Barbour Publishing, provided that the text does not exceed 500 words. When reproducing text from this book, include the following credit line: "From *Quick Bible Quizzes*, published by Barbour Publishing, Inc. Used by permission."

All scripture quotations are taken from the King James Version of the Bible.

Published by Barbour Publishing, Inc., 1810 Barbour Drive, Uhrichsville, Ohio 44683, www.barbourbooks.com

Our mission is to inspire the world with the life-changing message of the Bible.

Printed in the United States of America.

Introduction

**Sitting at the doctor's office. . .
standing in line at the BMV. . .waiting for
your train. . .why not take a quick test
of your biblical knowledge?**

Quick Bible Quizzes is a great way to pass time while polishing your memory of God's Word. These 300 quizzes, covering a wide range of topics, each contain five questions—long enough to engage your brain but short enough to finish before the deli calls your number!

On the pages to follow, you'll find quizzes with titles such as:

- Messianic Prophecies
- Raised from the Dead
- Birds of a Feather
- Grandpas
- God's Covenants
- Weirdest Things Eaten

The first quarter of the book tests your knowledge of broad themes. The rest of the book covers Bible history in basic, chronological order, starting with Creation and concluding with the New Jerusalem. Along the way, you'll test your knowledge of the famous and less well-known, in quizzes like:

- The First Sin
- Selling the Birthright
- David's Wives
- The Fishy Prophet

- Water into Wine
- Dorcas

All quizzes are based on the beloved King James Version of the Bible. And, of course, answers are provided, beginning on page 155.

Ready for a challenge? *Quick Bible Quizzes* entertains as it educates!

Quiz 1
Christmas

1. True or Trick: All four Gospels include some account of Jesus' birth.
2. Who did God send to tell Mary the news that she would give birth to Jesus?
3. After Jesus' birth, who were the first people to learn of it?
4. Who did the Holy Spirit promise would not see death before he saw the Lord's Messiah?
5. Fill in the Blank: "And when they had opened their treasures, they presented unto him gifts; _____, and frankincense and myrrh."

Quiz 2
Easter

1. Fill in the Blank: "And when they were come unto a place called _____, that is to say, a place of a skull."
2. While hanging on the cross, who did Jesus say was forsaking Him?
3. True or Trick: The soldiers forced Simon, a passerby, to carry Jesus' cross.
4. Who betrayed Jesus with a kiss?
5. Who was the first person Jesus showed Himself to after rising from the dead?

Quiz 3
Psalms

1. How many psalms are included in the book of Psalms?
2. Which Psalm did Moses write?
3. True or Trick: Jesus ended His ministry on earth by quoting from the Psalms.
4. Which Psalm does not end with hope or praise to God?
5. Fill in the Blank: "Thy _____ is a lamp unto my feet, and a light unto my path."

Quiz 4
Hands and Fingers

1. Fill in the Blank: "And he gave unto Moses...two tables of testimony, tables of stone, _____ with the finger of God."
2. Who said, "This is the finger of God"?
3. How many fingers did the Philistine giant at Gath have on each hand?
4. True or Trick: Once you have eternal life, no one can pluck you out of Jesus' hand.
5. When the Pharisees accused a woman caught in adultery, where did Jesus write with His finger?

Quiz 5
Salvation

1. Because salvation doesn't come through works, what can no one do in response?
2. Name one of two things one must do to be saved.
3. True or Trick: Salvation comes not by good deeds but by God's mercy, the washing of regeneration, and renewal from the Holy Ghost.
4. What did Jesus say He was the only way to?
5. Fill in the Blank: "Neither is there salvation in any other: for there is none other name under heaven given among _____, whereby we must be saved."

Quiz 6
Messianic Prophesies

1. Which prophet foretold Jesus' virgin birth?
2. Which prophet foretold Jesus would be born in Bethlehem?
3. Which prophet foretold Jesus would come riding on a donkey?
4. True or Trick: Jeremiah foretold that Jesus would be betrayed for thirty pieces of silver.
5. Fill in the Blank: "But he was wounded for our transgressions, he was _____ for our iniquities."

Quiz 7
Fish

1. On what day did God create the fish?
2. Where did the Israelites of Moses' day look back longingly for fish?
3. True or Trick: Because of Jonah's disobedience to God, God sent a great fish to swallow him up for a few days.
4. Name one of four of Jesus' disciples who were fishermen.
5. Fill in the Blank: "And he saith unto them, _____ me, and I will make you fishers of men."

Quiz 8
Weirdest Things Eaten

1. What did Moses grind to gold powder, mix with water, and make the Israelites drink?
2. True or Trick: A famine was once so great in Samaria that two women had resorted to eating their children.
3. Who did God command to eat a roll of a book with words of lament written on both sides?
4. What forbidden food caused the fall of humanity?
5. Fill in the Blank: "Then I took the little _____ out of the angel's hand, and ate it up; and it was in my mouth sweet as honey: and as soon as I had eaten it, my belly was bitter."

Quiz 9
Fun Facts

1. What is the longest chapter in the Bible?
2. What is the shortest chapter in the Bible?
3. What is the longest verse in the Bible?
4. True or Trick: The shortest verse in the King James Bible is 1 Thessalonians 5:16: "Rejoice evermore."
5. Fill in the Blank: "All scripture is given by inspiration of God, and is ____ for doctrine, for reproof, for correction, for instruction in righteousness."

Quiz 10
Riddles and Hard Sayings

1. Who gave a riddle in which the answer included "honey" and "lion"?
2. Fill in the Blank: "...to understand a ____, and the interpretation, the words of the wise, and their dark sayings."
3. In the Babylonian royal court, who was skilled in interpreting riddles and hard sentences?
4. True or Trick: God never speaks in riddles.
5. What was the reason God gave for speaking plainly to Moses?

Quiz 11
Famous Murderers

1. Who was the first murderer recorded in the Bible?

2. True or Trick: Abraham killed an Egyptian but later became one of the greatest leaders in Jewish history.

3. Which king had one of his soldiers murdered and then married the dead man's wife?

4. Fill in the Blank: "Then _____, when he saw that he was mocked of the wise men. . .slew all the children that were in Bethlehem. . .from two years old and under."

5. As a form of population control, who ordered all Hebrew boys to be killed?

Quiz 12
Our Adversary's Places of Abode

1. True or Trick: Before our adversary sinned, he walked among the stones of fire on the holy mountain of God.

2. Where is our adversary's kingdom right now?

3. After he's thrown out of heaven during the end times, where will our adversary be?

4. During Jesus' millennial reign on earth, where will our adversary be bound, locked, and sealed?

5. Fill in the Blank: "And the devil that deceived them was cast into the _____ of fire and brimstone. . .and shall be tormented day and night for ever and ever."

Quiz 13
Asking and Receiving

1. What must you do before God gives you the desires of your heart?
2. Who said, "Ask, and it shall be given you"?
3. True or Trick: Even if you doubt in prayer, you will receive.
4. What requests does God not grant?
5. Fill in the Blank: "Verily, verily, I say unto you, Whatsoever ye shall ask of the Father in my _____, he will give it you."

Quiz 14
Herbs and Spices

1. What appeared like coriander seed every morning for forty years in the wilderness?
2. Fill in the Blank: "Is there no balm in _____; is there no physician there?"
3. In what was Jesus' body wrapped along with some spices?
4. True or Trick: Jesus accused the Pharisees of tithing mint, anise, and cumin while omitting the weightier matters of the Law.
5. To what kind of seed did Jesus compare the kingdom of heaven?

Quiz 15
God's Voice

1. Who were the first people to hear God talking?

2. Which young boy kept hearing God calling his name one night?

3. To whom did God speak from atop Mt. Sinai?

4. True or Trick: The prophet Elijah heard God's still small voice.

5. Fill in the Blank: "And lo a voice from heaven, saying, This is my _____ Son, in whom I am well pleased."

Quiz 16
Cursed by God

1. What type of animal did God curse above all others?

2. Name one of two things God cursed the ground with.

3. True or Trick: Jesus cursed an apple tree for having no fruit.

4. Where is the curse not found?

5. Fill in the Blank: "Thus saith the Lord; Cursed be the man that trusteth in _____, and maketh flesh his arm, and whose heart departeth from the Lord."

Quiz 17
God's Word

1. Where did the scriptures originate?
2. How long will God's Word last?
3. True or Trick: It's good to adjust God's Word to the times by adapting or removing controversial verses.
4. What did Isaiah say God's Word would never do?
5. Fill in the Blank: "In the _____ was the Word, and the Word was with God, and the Word was God."

Quiz 18
Cows

1. Who dreamed that seven famished cows came out of a river and swallowed up seven well-fed cows?
2. Who made and worshipped a golden calf in the wilderness?
3. What color did Israel's sacrificial heifer have to be?
4. True or Trick: The Hittites returned the captured ark of the covenant in a cart pulled by two milk cows.
5. Fill in the Blank: "For every beast of the forest is mine, and the cattle upon a thousand _____."

Quiz 19
Stars in the Sky

1. Who did God promise would have as many descendants as there are stars in the sky?
2. Name one of two people who sang of how God used the stars to fight for them against Sisera.
3. Who followed a star to baby Jesus' location?
4. True or Trick: God has named every star in the sky.
5. Fill in the Blank: "When I _____ thy heavens, the work of thy fingers, the moon and the stars, which thou hast ordained. . ."

Quiz 20
Honey

1. What land flowed with milk and honey?
2. Who unknowingly broke King Saul's command by eating honey?
3. Who found a lion's carcass filled with honey and swarming with bees?
4. True or Trick: In a vision, John ate a book that was sweet like honey in his mouth but bitter in his stomach.
5. Fill in the Blank: "Pleasant _____ are as an honeycomb, sweet to the soul, and health to the bones."

Quiz 21
Fruit

1. What fruit of Canaan grew so big that it took two people to carry one cluster on a pole?
2. What fruit was put on King Hezekiah's boil for his recovery?
3. Oil from what fruit kept the tabernacle's lamps burning?
4. True or Trick: In heaven, the tree of life will bear twelve kinds of fruits.
5. Fill in the Blank: "A word fitly spoken is like _____ of gold in pictures of silver."

Quiz 22
Cups

1. Who dreamed that he pressed grapes into Pharaoh's cup?
2. Which son of Jacob found Joseph's silver cup in his sack of grain?
3. At the Last Supper, what did Jesus say the cup represented?
4. True or Trick: Just before He was arrested, Jesus prayed for His "cup" of suffering to be taken away.
5. Fill in the Blank: "Thou anointest my head with oil; my cup _____ over."

Quiz 23
Chariots

1. Who got into a chariot to go meet his father, whom he hadn't seen in years?

2. Who rode off into the sky in a chariot of fire?

3. Who was sitting in his chariot, reading from the prophet Isaiah?

4. True or Trick: Jehoiachin, a future king of Israel, was known for his "furious" chariot driving.

5. Fill in the Blank: "Some trust in chariots, and some in horses: but we will ____ the name of the LORD our God."

Quiz 24
Wind

1. Who looked for the Lord in a great strong wind but didn't find Him there?

2. True or Trick: After being awoken from a sound sleep on a storm-tossed boat, Jesus rebuked the wind and it stopped instantly.

3. Who came to the believers on Pentecost with a sound like a rushing mighty wind?

4. In John's vision of the future, who stood on the four corners of the earth and held the four winds?

5. Fill in the Blank: "The wind bloweth where it ____, and thou hearest the sound thereof, but canst not tell whence it cometh, and whither it goeth: so is every one that is born of the Spirit."

Quiz 25
Wells

1. After fleeing from Pharaoh, in what region did Moses sit down by a well?

2. Whom did God comfort by the well called Beerlahairoi?

3. Who found his future wife by a well when she came with his uncle's sheep?

4. True or Trick: Gideon had to dig three wells because the people of the land claimed the water was theirs.

5. Fill in the Blank: "Now Jacob's well was there. _____ therefore, being wearied with his journey, sat thus on the well: and it was about the sixth hour."

Quiz 26
Doors

1. What judge slew his enemy with his left hand, locked the doors behind him, and escaped before his enemy's servants could find a key?

2. What judge promised God that if He helped him win a battle, he'd offer whatever came through his doors as a burnt offering?

3. What judge carried a city gate's doors on his shoulders?

4. True or Trick: King Saul was so afraid of the king of Gath that he feigned madness, scrabbled on their doors, and drooled on his beard.

5. Fill in the Blank: "But the angel of the Lord by _____ opened the prison doors, and brought them forth."

Quiz 27
Hair

1. Whose strength from the Lord was preserved by not cutting his hair?

2. Who had so much hair that it weighed two hundred shekels every year when it was cut?

3. True or Trick: Just before going to Ephesus, Paul had his hair shaved off so as to not offend the Jews there.

4. In John's vision, whose hair was white as wool?

5. Fill in the Blank: "But the very hairs of your head are all _____."

Quiz 28
Windows

1. How many windows were in Noah's ark?

2. Who lived on the town wall and let two spies down by a cord through her window?

3. Who fell asleep listening to Paul preaching and fell out a window to his death?

4. True or Trick: King Abimelech was shocked to look out his window and see Isaac caressing his wife Rebekah, whom Isaac had claimed was his sister.

5. Fill in the Blank: "Jezebel heard of it; and she painted her _____, and tired her head, and looked out a window."

Quiz 29
Trees

1. What kind of tree was Aaron's staff made from?
2. True or Trick: King Solomon used the wood from cedar trees to build the Lord's temple.
3. Under what type of tree did a man of God sit after cursing King Jeroboam's altar?
4. What kind of tree did Zacchaeus climb so that he could see Jesus?
5. Fill in the Blank: "[The people] took branches of ____ trees, and went forth to meet him, and cried, Hosanna: Blessed is the King of Israel that cometh in the name of the Lord."

Quiz 30
Barley

1. What son of David set Joab's barley fields on fire to get his attention?
2. Who purchased a harlot to become his wife for fifteen pieces of silver and one and a half homers of barley?
3. True or Trick: Gideon overheard an enemy soldier telling his dream of a cake of barley bread that destroyed them.
4. Along with two fish, how many loaves of barley bread were used to feed five thousand people?
5. Fill in the Blank: "And now is not Boaz of our kindred. . . ? Behold, he ____ barley to night in the threshingfloor."

Quiz 31
Pools

1. True or Trick: King David hanged the bodies of two executed murderers over the pool in Hebron.

2. Which king's chariot, stained by his blood in battle, was washed at the pool of Samaria?

3. Which king made a pool and a conduit to bring water into Jerusalem?

4. Who stirred up the waters at the pool of Bethesda, bringing healing powers?

5. Fill in the Blank: "And said unto him, Go, wash in the pool of Siloam, (which is by interpretation, _____.)"

Quiz 32
Red

1. Who was born red and hairy?

2. What did the Israelites walk on when they passed through the Red Sea?

3. True or Trick: Dyed red rams' skins formed a cover for the Israelites' tabernacle.

4. In John's vision of the future, what power was given to the red horse?

5. Fill in the Blank: "Come now, and let us _____ together, saith the Lord: though your sins be as scarlet, they shall be white as snow; though they be red like crimson, they shall be as wool."

Quiz 33
Grass

1. On what day of creation did God create grass?

2. During the Samarian famine, who told Obadiah to go find grass for the horses and mules?

3. True or Trick: Because of King Saul's pride, God punished him by making him act like a beast and eat grass like an ox.

4. In John's vision, how much of the earth's green grass was burned up after the first angel sounded the trumpet?

5. Fill in the Blank: "The grass withereth, the flower ____: but the word of our God shall stand for ever."

Quiz 34
Shoes

1. Whom did God command to take off his shoes because he stood on holy ground?

2. As the Israelites prepared to leave Egypt, what did God tell the people to eat while wearing their shoes and holding their staffs?

3. With their old shoes and dry, moldy bread, who did the Gibeonites deceive into thinking they had come from afar?

4. True or Trick: The father was so overjoyed when his prodigal son came home that he ordered servants to bring shoes for his feet.

5. Fill in the Blank: "I indeed baptize you with water unto ____: but he that cometh after me is mightier than I, whose shoes I am not worthy to bear."

Quiz 35
You Bug Me!

1. When the people kept leftovers, what appeared in the manna the next day?

2. To what did most of the Israelite spies compare themselves when speaking of Canaan's giants?

3. Besides wild honey, what else did John the Baptist eat?

4. True or Trick: The writer of Proverbs tells the lazy to get their work ethic from the bees.

5. Fill in the Blank: "The _____ taketh hold with her hands, and is in kings' palaces."

Quiz 36
You Bug Me Again!

1. What was the fourth plague God inflicted on the Egyptians?

2. True or Trick: David asked King Saul why he'd waste his time chasing a flea.

3. What did God promise to send before the Israelites to drive out the people of Canaan?

4. Fill in the Blank: "Lay not up for yourselves treasures upon earth, where _____ and rust doth corrupt."

5. What insect did Jesus say the scribes and Pharisees strained out while they figuratively swallowed camels?

Quiz 37
Speaking of Camels...

1. While meditating in the field, who looked up to see his future wife riding a camel?
2. Who was sold by his brothers to a company of Ishmaelites who led camels carrying spices and balm?
3. True or Trick: Gideon took ornaments from the necks of his defeated enemy's camels.
4. Who came with camels carrying lots of gold, spices, and jewels to ask Solomon hard questions?
5. Fill in the Blank: "And again I say to you, It is easier for a camel to go through the ____ of a needle, than for a rich man to enter into the kingdom of God."

Quiz 38
Myrrh

1. Whose preparation to see her future husband involved six months with oil of myrrh?
2. For what did God want the combination of myrrh, cinnamon, calamus, cassia, and olive oil used?
3. Besides myrrh, what else did the wise men give baby Jesus?
4. True or Trick: While Jesus hung on the cross, soldiers offered Him water mixed with myrrh, but He refused it.
5. Fill in the Blank: "And there came also ____, which at the first came to Jesus by night, and brought a mixture of myrrh and aloes, about an hundred pound weight."

Quiz 39
Thrones

1. Which king had an ivory throne, overlaid with gold?

2. For whom did Solomon make a seat so she could sit at his right hand?

3. Which king on his throne arrogantly accepted his people's praise and was immediately smitten by the angel of the Lord?

4. True or Trick: In John's vision, there was a rainbow around God's throne.

5. Fill in the Blank: "The Lord is in his ____ temple, the Lord's throne is in heaven."

Quiz 40
Oil

1. In a parable of Jesus, how many foolish virgins forgot to bring oil while waiting for the bridegroom?

2. True or Trick: During a great famine, God blessed a widow, her son, and Elisha with a cruse of oil that never became empty.

3. In addition to oil, what did the "good Samaritan" pour on the injured man's wounds?

4. After dreaming of a ladder to heaven, who worshipped God by pouring oil over the stone he'd used as a pillow?

5. Fill in the Blank: "Then ____ took a vial of oil, and poured it upon his head, and kissed him, and said, Is it not because the Lord hath anointed thee. . . ?"

Quiz 41
Harps

1. Who was "the father of all such as handle the harp and organ"?

2. Who played his harp for Saul to soothe the king's soul?

3. Which newly anointed king briefly joined a company of prophets with their harps and other instruments?

4. True or Trick: In John's vision, those who were victorious over the beast stood on a sea of glass holding harps of God.

5. Fill in the Blank: "Praise the Lord with harp: _____ unto him with the psaltery."

Quiz 42
Sleep

1. Who had a tent peg nailed through his skull while he slept?

2. What prophet received a baked cake and water from God while he slept?

3. During a mighty storm on the Mediterranean, who was the only one sleeping on a ship headed to Tarshish?

4. True or Trick: Jesus slept on a pillow in a boat during a storm on the Sea of Galilee.

5. Fill in the Blank: "I laid me down and slept: I awaked; for the Lord _____ me."

Quiz 43
Sackcloth

1. What other substance often accompanies sackcloth in scripture?
2. True or Trick: When Elijah confronted Ahab with God's intended judgment on his family, he laughed and said maybe it's God who should wear sackcloth.
3. Whose edict caused Mordecai to grieve and wear sackcloth?
4. After hearing Jonah's message, the king of what city made every human and animal wear sackcloth?
5. Fill in the Blank: "For this gird you with sackcloth, lament and howl: for the fierce _____ of the LORD is not turned back from us."

Quiz 44
Robes

1. What king dressed in a robe of fine linen and went with the Levites as they brought the ark of the covenant to Jerusalem?
2. Who did King Ahab of Israel say should wear royal robes into battle while he himself would go disguised?
3. Which of his twelve sons did Jacob give a coat of many colors?
4. True or Trick: As part of their mockery of Jesus, Roman soldiers made Him wear a purple robe.
5. Fill in the Blank: "And _____ robes were given unto every one of them, and it was said unto them, that they should rest yet for a little season."

Quiz 45
Dancing

1. After the Israelites' victory over the Egyptians, who led the women in dancing and singing their praise to God?

2. Which king danced energetically before the ark of the covenant?

3. Who became jealous when women of Israel danced and sang about David's victory over Goliath?

4. True or Trick: When Moses came down from Mount Sinai with the Law, he found the Israelites dancing around a calf idol.

5. Fill in the Blank: "Thou hast turned for me my _____ into dancing."

Quiz 46
Baskets

1. In the dream of Pharaoh's chief baker, how many white baskets were on his head?

2. To whom did Gideon bring a basket of meat and unleavened cake?

3. True or Trick: After Jesus fed the five thousand, ten baskets of food remained.

4. Who was lowered over the city wall in a basket at night because men sought to kill him at the gates?

5. Fill in the Blank: "And when she could not longer hide him, she took for him an ark [basket] of bulrushes, and daubed it with slime and with _____, and put the child therein; and she laid it in the flags by the river's brink."

Quiz 47
Salt

1. When God destroyed Sodom and Gomorrah, who was turned into a pillar of salt?

2. True or Trick: God commanded that every meat offering be seasoned with salt.

3. Who killed everyone in Shechem, beat down the city, and sowed it with salt?

4. Who healed a city's waters by throwing salt into the spring?

5. Fill in the Blank: "Ye are the salt of the ____: but if the salt have lost his savour, wherewith shall it be salted?"

Quiz 48
Clouds

1. True or Trick: On the day the tabernacle was set up in the wilderness, a cloud covered it.

2. While Elijah prayed for rain, how many times did he send his servant to look toward the sea before the servant finally saw a cloud?

3. Who did Jesus say everyone would see coming in the clouds of heaven?

4. Who will believers meet in the air at the end of time?

5. Fill in the Blank: "Who layeth the beams of his chambers in the waters: who maketh the clouds his ____: who walketh upon the wings of the wind."

Quiz 49
Writing

1. Who literally wrote the ten commandments?
2. Who wrote "Mene, Mene, Tekel, Upharsin" on Belshazzar's wall?
3. Who was the mute father who wrote his newborn son's name on a writing tablet?
4. True or Trick: Pilate wrote "Jesus of Nazareth, The King of the Jews" and put it on the cross.
5. Fill in the Blank: "And it came to pass, when ____ had made an end of writing the words of this law in a book, until they were finished."

Quiz 50
Time

1. How does the Lord view a thousand years?
2. For what purpose did God appoint the moon?
3. True or Trick: According to God, tomorrow is the accepted time and day of salvation.
4. To illustrate how short life is, what does James compare it to?
5. Fill in the Blank: "To every thing there is a season, and a time to every ____ under the heaven."

Quiz 51
Seven

1. Who blessed and sanctified the seventh day?
2. Who had seven demons cast out of her by Jesus?
3. When Elijah sent his servant seven times toward the sea, what did his servant finally see?
4. True or Trick: Jacob loved Leah so much that he agreed to work seven years to marry her.
5. Fill in the Blank: "[The angel] cried with a loud voice, as when a lion roareth: and when he had cried, seven _____ uttered their voices."

Quiz 52
Lions

1. Which of the twelve tribes of Israel is known as a lion?
2. As a shepherd, who killed both a lion and a bear to save his sheep?
3. True or Trick: God sent a lion to kill a prophet because of his disobedience, and the lion stood by the man's donkey until someone came to bury him.
4. Who was attacked by a lion while walking to Timnah?
5. Fill in the Blank: "Be sober, be vigilant; because your adversary the devil, as a roaring lion, walketh about, _____ whom he may devour."

Quiz 53
Sheep

1. Who is the first recorded shepherd in the Bible?

2. True or trick: Moses used green poplar, hazel, and chestnut trees to make sure his sheep and goats were born speckled and spotted?

3. Where did Abraham see a ram when he was about to sacrifice Isaac?

4. To whom did Nathan tell a parable about a rich man who took a poor man's only lamb?

5. Fill in the Blank: "All we like sheep have gone _____; we have turned every one to his own way; and the Lord hath laid on him the iniquity of us all."

Quiz 54
Thieves

1. Who took the ark of God and put it in the house of their false god Dagon?

2. People from which tribe of Israel stole valuable items and even a priest from Micah's house?

3. Who stole both his brother's birthright and his blessing?

4. True or Trick: Rachel stole her father's idols when Jacob moved his family away from Laban.

5. Fill in the Blank: "The thief cometh not, but for to steal, and to kill, and to _____: I am come that they might have life."

Quiz 55
Brass

1. Who was blinded, bound in brass chains, and carried to Babylon?

2. True or Trick: If the Israelites didn't obey God, He promised to make the sky like brass so that no rain would come.

3. Whose coat of mail weighed five thousand shekels of brass?

4. What type of animal did God command Moses to make out of brass and hang on a pole?

5. Fill in the Blank: "Thy _____ shall be iron and brass; and as thy days, so shall thy strength be."

Quiz 56
Teeth

1. What type of meat was still in the Israelites' teeth when God put a plague on them for complaining?

2. True or Trick: David had such woes that he said his bone stuck to his skin and he escaped by the skin of his teeth.

3. In Daniel's vision of four beasts, the bear had three of what between its teeth?

4. As Jeremiah lamented the destruction of Jerusalem, what did he say broke his teeth?

5. Fill in the Blank: "And shall cast them into a furnace of fire: there shall be _____ and gnashing of teeth."

Quiz 57
Beards

1. When David's servants were mistaken for spies, what did his enemies do to their beards?

2. The psalmist said that anointing oil ran down whose beard?

3. In a show of concern over Absalom's coup, who stopped washing his clothes and trimming his beard until David returned?

4. True or Trick: Isaiah foretold that people would hit Jesus' face and pluck out His beard.

5. Fill in the Blank: "And when I heard this thing, I rent my garment and my mantle, and _____ off the hair of my head and of my beard, and sat down astonied."

Quiz 58
Posts

1. What was each Israelite to smear on his lintel and his two side posts so that God would spare the firstborn in that house?

2. What was to be written on the posts of each Israelite house?

3. True or Trick: Samson threw the doors of the city gate and its two posts into a river.

4. Who saw the posts of the temple's doors shake when the seraphims shouted, "Holy, holy, holy, is the LORD of hosts"?

5. Fill in the Blank: "Blessed is the man that heareth me [wisdom], watching daily at my _____, waiting at the posts of my doors."

Quiz 59
Eyes

1. True or Trick: When regarding a person, man looks at the outward appearance, but God looks at the heart.

2. When Elisha prayed for God to open his servant's eyes, what did the young man see?

3. What did a blind man see at first when Jesus began healing him?

4. What fell from the newly-converted Saul's eyes so that he could see again?

5. Fill in the Blank: "_____ thou mine eyes, that I may behold wondrous things out of thy law."

Quiz 60
Nostrils

1. When did man become a living soul?

2. When the Flood came, who died?

3. Who said the spirit of God was in his nostrils?

4. True or Trick: God was angry with the Israelites' complaining, so He made them eat quail for a month until it came out of their nostrils.

5. Fill in the Blank: "By the _____ of God they perish, and by the breath of his nostrils are they consumed."

Quiz 61
Crowns

1. What type of crown do we receive for living for Christ every day?

2. True or Trick: There will be a special crown for those who see the fruit of their witnessing.

3. What type of crown does one get for longing for Christ's appearance?

4. What type of crown is reserved for the shepherds of God's flocks?

5. Fill in the Blank: "Blessed is the man that endureth temptation: for when he is tried, he shall receive the crown of ____."

Quiz 62
Barren Women

1. True or Trick: When neither Sarah nor Rebekah could bear children, Abraham prayed for Sarah, but Isaac took matters into his own hands.

2. Who remained barren because her sister was not loved?

3. Who was barren until she finally gave birth to Samson, the future judge?

4. Who was barren until finally she gave birth to Samuel, the future prophet?

5. Fill in the Blank: "And [Zacharias] had no child, because that ____ was barren, and they both were now well stricken in years."

Quiz 63
Birds of a Feather

1. On which day of creation did God create birds?
2. After the ark rested on the mountains of Ararat, what type of bird did Noah release first?
3. True or Trick: The eagle is one of the birds God declares unclean.
4. Fill in the Blank: "Fear ye not therefore, ye are of more value than many _____."
5. Among other things, what kind of bird was delivered by ships of Tharshish to King Solomon every three years?

Quiz 64
Grandpas

1. Who was the grandfather to King David's father, Jesse?
2. True or Trick: Methuselah was Noah's grandpa.
3. Who was Jacob's grandpa?
4. Name three of Isaac's twelve grandsons.
5. Fill in the blank: "And Terah took Abram his son, and _____ the son of Haran his son's son, and Sarai his daughter in law, his son Abram's wife; and they went forth with them from Ur of the Chaldees."

Quiz 65
Quakes and Twisters and Hail—Oh My!

1. True or Trick: The earth swallowed the rebels from Keturah's tribe alive, along with all their possessions.

2. Fill in the Blank: "There came a great _____ from the wilderness, and smote the four corners of the house, and it fell upon [Job's children], and they are dead."

3. What was the seventh plague on Egypt?

4. What natural phenomenon destroyed five pagan armies as they fled from Joshua and the Israelites?

5. What phenomenon occurred as soon as Jesus gave up His spirit on the cross?

Quiz 66
Inns

1. Who found a man robbed and beaten, gave him some first aid, and brought him to an inn to recover?

2. True or Trick: David and his men found their money in the grain sacks they'd paid for when they stopped at an inn to feed their donkeys.

3. Whom did the Lord almost kill by an inn because his son wasn't circumcised?

4. Who laid her firstborn son in a manger because there was no room in the inn?

5. What prostitute of Jericho lodged two Israelite spies in her home?

Quiz 67
Raised From the Dead

1. With God's help, who raised Tabitha (or Dorcas) from the dead?

2. With God's help, who raised a widow's son from the dead in the Old Testament?

3. With God's help, who raised Eutychus from the dead after he fell from a window?

4. True or Trick: A man rose from the dead when his body touched Elisha's bones.

5. Fill in the Blank: "[Jesus said,] Lazarus, come forth. And he that was dead came forth, bound hand and foot with graveclothes: and his _____ was bound about with a napkin."

Quiz 68
Kings

1. Which king of Judah had the longest reign (fifty-five years)?

2. True or Trick: Israel's King Zimri reigned for only seven days.

3. Who was the youngest king, crowned at age seven?

4. What king reigned in Hebron and then in Jerusalem?

5. Fill in the Blank: "And the Lord said unto Samuel. . . they have _____ me, that I should not reign over them."

Quiz 69
False Gods

1. What stone idol fell before the ark of the Lord two nights in a row?

2. True or Trick: Those who worship idols become as deaf and blind as the idols themselves.

3. Fill in the Blank: "Thou shalt not make unto thee any _____ image."

4. In the wilderness, the Israelites crafted their idol into what animal?

5. What king removed his own mother from leadership for erecting an idol?

Quiz 70
Flowers

1. Fill in the Blank: "I am the _____ of Sharon, and the lily of the valleys."

2. Which flower did Jesus say was more beautiful than King Solomon dressed in his finest clothes?

3. True or Trick: Inside Solomon's temple were open flower blossoms carved from cedar.

4. Whose rod budded with blossoms and almonds at night?

5. Unlike the grass and the flower, which wither and fade, what will last forever?

Quiz 71
Smoke, Clouds, and Fire

1. True or Trick: God appeared to Jacob as a burning lamp and a smoking furnace.
2. Who saw God appearing as a fire in a bush?
3. To whom did God appear as a pillar of cloud by day and a pillar of fire by night?
4. What did God the Holy Ghost appear as on the day of Pentecost?
5. Fill in the Blank: "And the house was filled with the cloud, and the court was full of the _____ of the Lord's glory."

Quiz 72
God's Covenants

1. What did God promise Adam and Eve in the garden of Eden?
2. What did God promise Noah to never do again?
3. True or Trick: God promised Abraham a land, a great nation, blessings, and eternal security.
4. What did God promise King David?
5. Fill in the Blank: "For this is my _____ of the new testament, which is shed for many for the remission of sins."

Quiz 73
Creation

1. How many days did God use to create everything?
2. True or Trick: God considered all of His created things "very good."
3. How did God create mankind, which differed from all the other living things?
4. On which day of creation did God make man?
5. Fill in the Blank: "And God blessed them, and God said unto them, Be fruitful, and multiply, and replenish the earth, and _____ it."

Quiz 74
What a Woman!

1. Fill in the Blank: "And the LORD God said, It is not good that the man should be _____."
2. What two-word phrase did God say He would provide for Adam?
3. True or Trick: God caused Eve to rise up out of the ground.
4. Why was Adam's wife called "Eve"?
5. Fill in the Blank: "And they were both _____, the man and his wife, and were not ashamed."

Quiz 75
The First Sin

1. Who tempted Eve to sin?
2. What type of plant contained the knowledge of good and evil in the garden of Eden?
3. Fill in the Blank: "And they sewed _____ leaves together, and made themselves aprons."
4. True or Trick: God cursed the ground with thorns and thistles because of Adam's sin.
5. What kind of sword did God's appointed cherubim use to guard the garden's entrance?

Quiz 76
The First Murder

1. True or Trick: Cain was a keeper of swine.
2. What was Abel's occupation?
3. Which of the brothers' offering did the Lord accept?
4. Where did Cain murder Abel?
5. Fill in the Blank: "And if thou doest not well, _____ lieth at the door. And unto thee shall be his desire, and thou shalt rule over him."

Quiz 77
Noah

1. How many decks did the ark have?
2. How old was Noah when the Flood came?
3. Fill in the Blank: "And the rain was upon the _____ forty days and forty nights."
4. True or Trick: There was so much water that it covered even the mountains.
5. After the waters receded, where did the ark land?

Quiz 78
The Tower of Babel

1. True or Trick: At one point in human history, everyone spoke the same language.
2. What did the people of Babel fear?
3. Fill in the Blank: "Let us build us a _____ and a tower, whose top may reach unto heaven."
4. How did God stop the people's plans?
5. In what land was the unfinished city of Babel located?

Quiz 79
Abraham

1. How old was Abraham when he had Isaac?

2. Before Abraham had a son, who was going to be his heir?

3. Fill in the Blank: "Is any thing too _____ for the LORD? At the time appointed I will return unto thee, according to the time of life, and Sarah shall have a son."

4. True or Trick: Isaac was Abraham's firstborn.

5. Who was the priest to whom Abraham gave a tithe?

Quiz 80
Lot and Abraham Separate

1. True or Trick: Because of a strife between Abraham and Lot, they chose to part ways.

2. Why was the land not able to bear Abraham and Lot?

3. Where did Lot choose to live?

4. Where did Abraham choose to live?

5. Fill in the Blank: "If thou wilt take the left hand, then I will go to the right; or if thou _____ to the right hand, then I will go to the left."

Quiz 81
Abraham's Sons

1. Who was the mother of Ishmael, Abraham's first son?
2. How many descendants did God promise to Abraham?
3. True or Trick: Abraham was 120 years old when his second son Isaac was born.
4. With God's promise of blessing, what did Abraham do with Ishmael and his mother after Isaac was born?
5. Fill in the Blank: "And in thee shall all families of the earth be ____."

Quiz 82
Sodom and Gomorrah

1. Who were the guests Lot invited to his place?
2. How did Lot's guests punish all the men of Sodom who demanded to "know" them?
3. As Lot and his family escaped, what was the one direction they were not to look?
4. True or Trick: Lot's wife disobeyed orders and was instantly turned into a pillar of salt.
5. Fill in the Blank: "And he looked toward Sodom and Gomorrah...and, lo, the smoke of the country went up as the smoke of a ____."

Quiz 83
Talk about a Sacrifice!

1. True or Trick: At first, Abraham debated God's command to sacrifice his son Isaac.

2. In what land did God command Abraham to sacrifice Isaac?

3. What did Abraham do to Isaac before placing him on the altar?

4. At the last second, what animal did God provide in place of Isaac?

5. Fill in the Blank: "For because thou has done this thing, and hast not withheld thy son, thine only son: that in _____ I will bless thee."

Quiz 84
Rebekah

1. Who was Rebekah's husband?

2. From what people was Abraham's servant *not* to look for a wife?

3. True or Trick: The sign for which Abraham's servant asked God was a woman who'd draw water from the well for both him and his camels.

4. Who was Rebekah's brother?

5. Fill in the Blank: "And they blessed Rebekah, and said unto her, Thou art our sister, be thou the _____ of thousands of millions."

Quiz 85
Selling the Birthright

1. True or Trick: Isaac favored Jacob, but Rebekah favored Esau.
2. What was Esau's main pursuit?
3. Which brother despised his birthright?
4. What was the family birthright sold for?
5. Fill in the Blank: "Behold, I am at the point to _____: and what profit shall this birthright do to me?"

Quiz 86
Stolen Blessing

1. What was Isaac's ailment which aided Jacob's deception?
2. Who overheard Isaac's instructions to Esau?
3. Name one of two things Isaac checked for in order to ensure he was blessing Esau.
4. True or Trick: Isaac was confused because he heard Jacob's voice but everything else seemed to be Esau.
5. Fill in the Blank: "Hast thou but _____ blessing, my father? bless me, even me also, O my father. And Esau lifted up his voice, and wept."

Quiz 87
Jacob's Ladder

1. When did Jacob see this ladder?
2. Who was going up and down this ladder?
3. True or Trick: The lower end of the ladder rested on the clouds and the upper end reached to heaven.
4. What did Jacob rename this place, originally called Luz?
5. Fill in the Blank: "And he was ____, and said, How dreadful is this place! this is none other but the house of God, and this is the gate of heaven."

Quiz 88
The Case of the Two Wives

1. Which of his wives did Jacob love more?
2. Who tricked Jacob into marrying the wrong sister?
3. What did both women do when they couldn't bear children?
4. True or Trick: Ultimately Jacob had a total of twelve sons.
5. Fill in the Blank: "And God said unto him, I am God Almighty: be fruitful and ____: a nation and a company of nations shall be of thee."

Quiz 89
Dinah

1. True or Trick: Dinah was Isaac's daughter.
2. What prince raped Dinah?
3. What did both the prince and his father want Dinah to do?
4. Which two brothers of Dinah sought to avenge her?
5. Fill in the Blank: "Jacob said. . .Ye have troubled me to make me to _____ among the inhabitants of the land."

Quiz 90
Joseph's Dreams

1. How many dreams did Joseph have?
2. What were all the object in Joseph's dreams doing?
3. True or Trick: Joseph's brothers grudgingly accepted him after hearing his dreams.
4. What did Joseph's father, Jacob, do when he heard the dream?
5. Fill in the Blank: "And [Joseph] said unto them, _____, I pray you, this dream which I have dreamed."

Quiz 91
Joseph Sold into Slavery

1. Which of Joseph's brothers suggested throwing him into a pit instead of killing him?

2. Which brother said they should sell Joseph as a slave?

3. True or Trick: Joseph's brothers sold him to Egyptian traders.

4. For how many pieces of silver was Joseph sold?

5. Fill in the Blank: "And they took Joseph's coat, and killed a kid of the _____, and dipped the coat in the blood."

Quiz 92
Joseph's Owner, Potiphar

1. Fill in the Blank: "And the Lord was with Joseph, and he was a _____ man."

2. Why did Potiphar's wife want to sleep with Joseph?

3. True or Trick: One day, Joseph fled from the woman's grasp so fast that he left his garment in her hand.

4. What was Joseph's punishment after he was falsely accused of attempted rape?

5. Who showed Joseph mercy and gave him favor with the warden?

Quiz 93
Prisoner Dreams

1. Name one of the two prisoners from Pharaoh's court.
2. What did the three branches and baskets in the dreams represent?
3. Of the two dreams, how many did Joseph accurately interpret?
4. True or Trick: One prisoner was so happy that he couldn't stop talking about Joseph.
5. Fill in the Blank: "And Joseph said unto them, Do not ____ belong to God? tell me them, I pray you."

Quiz 94
Job the Blessed

1. In what region did Job live?
2. How many children did Job have?
3. True or Trick: Job's daughters would eat at a different son's house every day of the week.
4. What did Job do in the morning on behalf of each of his children?
5. Fill in the Blank: "And that man was perfect and upright, and one that ____ God, and eschewed evil."

Quiz 95
Job's First Test

1. Who presented themselves before the Lord?
2. True or Trick: God let Satan touch everything that belonged to Job except his health.
3. What happened to Job's camels?
4. What killed Job's children?
5. Fill in the Blank: "Naked came I out of my mother's womb, and naked shall I return thither: the Lord gave, and the Lord hath taken away; _____ be the name of the Lord."

Quiz 96
Job's Second Test

1. Where does Satan go to and fro?
2. What did God allow Satan to destroy in Job's second test?
3. True or Trick: Job's wife reminded him they both still needed to trust God in all this.
4. How many friends came to mourn with Job and comfort him?
5. Fill in the Blank: "And he took him a potsherd to scrape himself withal; and he sat down among the _____."

Quiz 97
Miserable Comforters

1. True or Trick: Job's three friends assumed his suffering was caused by his sins.
2. When God finally spoke to Job, where did the voice come from?
3. Name one of the two star constellations which God mentioned to Job.
4. What did God tell Job's three friends to do?
5. Fill in the Blank: "I know that thou canst do every thing, and that no _____ can be withholden from thee."

Quiz 98
The End of Job's Story

1. True or Trick: The Lord blessed Job with twice as much as he had before.
2. Name one of two things Job's kinsmen and friends each gave him.
3. How beautiful were each of Job's daughters?
4. How many more years did Job live?
5. Fill in the Blank: "So the Lord _____ the latter end of Job more than his beginning."

Quiz 99
Baby Moses

1. From what tribe did Moses hail?
2. How old was Moses when he was put into a basket to float in the river?
3. True or Trick: Pharaoh's daughter named him Moses because she drew him out of water.
4. Who was Moses' wet nurse?
5. Fill in the Blank: "And his _____ stood afar off, to wit what would be done to him."

Quiz 100
Moses the Young Man

1. True or Trick: Moses was a murderer.
2. How many daughters did the priest of Midian—Moses' future father-in-law—have?
3. Fill in the Blank: "And Moses was content to dwell with the man: and he gave Moses _____ his daughter."
4. What was the name of Moses' firstborn son?
5. Why did God hear the children of Israel groaning?

Quiz 101
Moses the Shepherd

1. What was the name of the mountain of God to which Moses led his father-in-law's flock?
2. What did Moses see burning with fire but not consumed?
3. What did Moses do when God spoke?
4. True or Trick: Moses kept saying no to God's command to return to Egypt and face Pharaoh.
5. Fill in the Blank: "Now therefore go, and I will be with thy ____, and teach thee what thou shalt say."

Quiz 102
Moses, God's Spokesman

1. True or Trick: Moses left his wife and sons with Jethro, his father-in-law, while he returned to Egypt.
2. On the way back to Egypt, who sought to kill Moses?
3. Whom did Moses meet in the wilderness on his way back to Egypt?
4. Did the Israelites believe everything that was told to them?
5. Fill in the Blank: "See that thou do all those wonders before Pharaoh, which I have put in thine hand: but I will ____ his heart, that he shall not let the people go."

Quiz 103
The Ten Plagues

1. In the first plague, what did God turn Egypt's water into?
2. Who couldn't stand before Moses because of the boils?
3. Who hardened Pharaoh's heart?
4. Fill in the Blank: "And Moses stretched forth his hand toward heaven; and there was a thick darkness in all the land of Egypt _____ days."
5. True or Trick: In the tenth plague, the Lord spared the firstborn of all livestock.

Quiz 104
Tabernacle Items

1. Name one of two furnishings in the outer court of the tabernacle.
2. What was the one thing inside the tabernacle that held edible food?
3. What was the only thing inside the tabernacle that emitted light?
4. True or Trick: Just in front of the veil to the most holy place was the ark of the covenant.
5. Fill in the Blank: "And thou shalt make an altar to burn _____ upon: of shittim wood shalt thou make it."

Quiz 105
Tabernacle and Temple Offerings

1. Which voluntary offering was to be from the herd or flock?
2. True or Trick: A meat offering included pouring oil and frankincense over fine flour.
3. Upon what were offerings to be burned?
4. For the sin offering, what was the priest to take from the camp and pour out?
5. Fill in the Blank: "And he shall bring his trespass offering unto the LORD for his sin. . .and the priest shall make an _____ for him concerning his sin."

Quiz 106
The Twelve Spies

1. What land were the spies searching?
2. How many people were needed to carry one huge cluster of grapes?
3. True or Trick: The spies reported that the land ate the people and that the inhabitants were giants.
4. How many of the twelve spies trusted in God's promise rather than the terrifying sights?
5. Fill in the Blank: "If the LORD delight in us, then he will _____ us into this land, and give it us; a land which floweth with milk and honey."

Quiz 107
Fiery Serpents Incident

1. For what sin did the Lord send fiery serpents to kill some of His people?
2. Fill in the Blank: "And the Lord sent fiery serpents among the people, and they bit the people; and much people of Israel _____."
3. After the fiery serpents started killing people, what did the people ask Moses to do?
4. Who suggested making a serpent of brass and lifting it up on a pole?
5. True or Trick: Those who were bitten by a serpent just had to look at the brass serpent to live.

Quiz 108
Balaam

1. True or Trick: Balak, the king of the Amorites, was terrified of the Israelites and their Lord, so he hired Balaam to curse them.
2. Who told Balaam that he could not curse the Israelites?
3. What animal miraculously spoke to Balaam?
4. Who was standing on the road, sword drawn, ready to kill Balaam?
5. Fill in the Blank: "I have _____; for I knew not that thou stoodest in the way against me: now therefore, if it displease thee, I will get me back again."

Quiz 109
Rahab

1. How many spies did Rahab hide?

2. Where in her home did Rahab hide the spies?

3. True or Trick: The spies made an unconditional promise that the Israelite army would spare Rahab.

4. What was Rahab supposed to display in her window?

5. Fill in the Blank: "And she said unto the men, I know that the Lord hath given you the land, and that your ____ is fallen upon us."

Quiz 110
Crossing the Jordan

1. When would God make a dry path though the Jordan river for the Israelites?

2. True or Trick: The Jordan river was overflowing its banks because it always did so during the harvest season.

3. Where did the priests stand while everyone crossed the river?

4. How many stones were carried from the dry path in the river and used as a memorial?

5. Fill in the Blank: "On that day the Lord magnified ____ in the sight of all Israel."

Quiz 111
The Walls of Jericho

1. How many times were the Israelites to walk around Jericho for each of the first six days?
2. True or Trick: On the seventh day, the priests blew trumpets and the people shouted, "Holy, Holy, Holy."
3. How were the Israelites to communicate before they shouted?
4. Who from Jericho was saved with Rahab?
5. Fill in the Blank: "And the people shouted with a great shout, that the wall fell down _____."

Quiz 112
Achan

1. What sin did Achan commit?
2. What was Achan's punishment?
3. True or Trick: Because of Achan's sin, the Israelite army was defeated by their enemy.
4. What was the name of the enemy the Israelites battled against?
5. Fill in the Blank: "Neither will I be with you any more, except ye _____ the accursed from among you."

Quiz 113
Deception!

1. Who deceived Joshua and the Israelites into making a peace treaty with them?

2. True or Trick: These people used moldy bread and old sacks, shoes, and clothes to make it look like they'd traveled a long distance.

3. How long did it take Joshua and the Israelites to realize the truth?

4. Why couldn't the Israelites kill these people?

5. Fill in the Blank: "And Joshua called for them. . .saying, Wherefore have ye _____ us, saying, We are very far from you; when ye dwell among us?"

Quiz 114
An *Un*natural Phenomenon

1. True or Trick: Five Canaanite cities joined forces to fight against Jerusalem.

2. What did the Lord throw down from heaven at the enemy armies?

3. For what did Joshua pray during the battle?

4. When did nature return to normal?

5. Fill in the Blank: "And there was no day like that before it or after it, that the Lord hearkened unto the _____ of a man."

Quiz 115
Ehud

1. What pagan king ruled over Israel before God called Ehud as judge?
2. What less-common trait is noted by scripture regarding Ehud?
3. True or Trick: After Ehud killed the enemy king, he made his escape because the king's servants were too ashamed to peek into his quiet locked room.
4. How many enemy soldiers did Ehud and the Israelites kill?
5. Fill in the Blank: "And he said unto them, Follow me: for the Lord hath delivered your enemies the _____ into your hands."

Quiz 116
Deborah and Barak

1. How many years did Jabin and his army oppress Israel?
2. Under what type of tree did Deborah dwell when she judged?
3. Fill in the Blank: "And Deborah said unto Barak, Up; for this is the _____ in which the Lord hath delivered Sisera into thine hand."
4. Who gave Sisera milk and a place to rest when he was being chased?
5. True or Trick: Sisera died after a tent nail was hammered into his head while he slept.

Quiz 117
Gideon's Wet Blanket

1. Why was Gideon threshing wheat in the winepress?

2. What did the Lord command Gideon to do?

3. True or Trick: The Lord chose Gideon because he was the firstborn from a strong family.

4. How many times did Gideon use a fleece to ask for proof of his calling?

5. Fill in the Blank: "And the angel of the Lord appeared unto him, and said unto him, The Lord is with thee, thou mighty man of ____."

Quiz 118
God Handpicks Gideon's Army

1. What was Gideon's other name?

2. How many times did God whittle down Gideon's army?

3. True or Trick: God told Gideon that only those men who lapped up water like a dog could remain in the army.

4. How many men did God finally allow in Gideon's army?

5. Fill in the Blank: "And the Lord said unto Gideon, The people that are with thee are too ____ for me to give the Midianites into their hands."

Quiz 119
The Battle That Never Actually Occurred

1. Into how many companies did Gideon divide his men?
2. Name one of the three items every man carried with him.
3. True or Trick: The army used the lamps to light the enemy's tents on fire.
4. How did God defeat the enemy?
5. Fill in the Blank: "Arise; for the Lord hath delivered into your hand the host of ____."

Quiz 120
Samson and Delilah

1. True or Trick: The Philistines asked Delilah to find out where Samson's strength was so that they could capture him.
2. How many pieces of silver did each Philistine promise to give Delilah?
3. How many times did Samson trick her?
4. What was Samson since before birth, which explains why his hair was never cut?
5. Fill in the Blank: "He wist not that the Lord was ____ from him."

Quiz 121
Samson the Prisoner

1. What violent act did the Philistines commit on Samson?

2. True or Trick: The Philistines crowded into their temple to thank their god Ashtoreth for delivering their enemy Samson to them.

3. What did Samson push over to destroy the temple?

4. How many years did Samson judge Israel?

5. Fill in the Blank: "And Samson called unto the LORD, and said, O Lord God, remember me, I pray thee, and _____ me, I pray thee, only this once, O God."

Quiz 122
Ruth

1. Who was Ruth's mother-in-law?

2. What nationality was Ruth?

3. True or Trick: Ruth met her future second husband while gathering fallen grain on his property.

4. Fill in the Blank: "For wither thou goest, I will go; and where thou lodgest, I will lodge: thy people shall be my people, and thy _____ my _____." (same word for both blanks)

5. Where did Ruth sleep while she waited for Boaz to wake up so that she could ask him to marry her?

Quiz 123
Hannah

1. Why was Hannah crying so much?
2. While Hannah was deep in prayer at the Lord's tabernacle, what did Eli the priest think of her?
3. True or Trick: God answered her prayer with a daughter, followed by a son a year later.
4. What did Hannah do with her little boy once he was weaned?
5. Fill in the Blank: "There is none holy as the Lord: for there is none beside thee: neither is there any _____ like our God."

Quiz 124
Samuel's Call

1. At what time of day did God call Samuel?
2. At first, who did Samuel think was speaking?
3. True or Trick: God had to call Samuel three times before Samuel replied to Him.
4. Fill in the Blank: "_____; for thy servant heareth."
5. Who did God tell young Samuel that He was about to judge?

Quiz 125
Captured Ark

1. Who captured the ark of the Lord while battling against the Israelites?

2. True or Trick: When the false idol Baal fell down the second time before the ark of the Lord, his stone head and hands broke off.

3. Why did God's enemies keep moving the ark from city to city?

4. What did the captors ultimately decide to do with the ark of the Lord?

5. Fill in the Blank: "And the men that died not were smitten with the _____: and the cry of the city went up to heaven."

Quiz 126
Returned Ark

1. True or Trick: The ark of the Lord was returned in a new cart, pulled by two cows that had never been yoked.

2. What historical event caused the captors to return the ark of the Lord?

3. To what city was the ark of the Lord returned?

4. Why did the Lord kill seventy Israelite men?

5. Fill in the Blank: "Who is able to stand before this _____ Lord God? and to whom shall he go up from us?

Quiz 127
Israel's First King

1. Who was anointed as the first king of Israel?
2. What did the future king's father lose which caused the young man to end up meeting Samuel?
3. True or Trick: The future king was very short.
4. When it came time to publicly present the first king to Israel, where was he?
5. Fill in the Blank: "And ye [Israelites] have this day ____ your God, who himself saved you out of all your adversities and your tribulations."

Quiz 128
Jabesh-Gilead

1. What were the terms of Nahash the Ammonite's treaty with the people in Jabesh-Gilead?
2. How long did the people asked Nahash to wait before carrying out his threat?
3. Fill in the Blank: "And the Spirit of God came upon ____ when he heard those tidings, and his anger was kindled greatly."
4. At what time of day did all of Israel come to Jabesh-Gilead's defense?
5. True or Trick: There were no survivors from Nahash's army.

Quiz 129
The Giant

1. For whom was the giant Goliath fighting?
2. How many days did Goliath taunt the Israelite army?
3. How many stones did it take for David to kill Goliath?
4. Fill in the Blank: "Thou comest to me with a sword, and with a spear, and with a shield: but I come to thee in the name of the Lord of ____, the God of the armies of Israel."
5. True or Trick: David used his own sword to cut off Goliath's head.

Quiz 130
David's Wives

1. True or Trick: David's first wife was Michal, daughter of King Saul.
2. Which of David's wives was the widow of the scoundrel Nabal, whom the Lord killed?
3. Which wife did David commit adultery with before he married her?
4. Out of all of David's wives, which one gave birth to King Solomon?
5. Fill in the Blank: "And David said unto Nathan, I have sinned against the Lord. And Nathan said unto David, The Lord also hath put away thy sin; thou shalt not ____."

Quiz 131
David Spares Saul's Life

1. How many men did King Saul take with him to pursue David?

2. True or Trick: When Saul went in a cave to cover his feet (or relieve himself), David and his men were there.

3. What did David do instead of killing Saul?

4. How did Saul describe David when he learned about David's opportunity to kill him?

5. Fill in the Blank: "The Lord judge between me and thee, and the Lord avenge me of thee: but mine _____ shall not be upon thee."

Quiz 132
Woman with a Familiar Spirit

1. In what city did the woman with the familiar spirit live?

2. True or Trick: King Saul disguised himself when he went to this woman.

3. Whom did Saul want brought up from the dead?

4. Where did the spirit say Saul and his sons would be the next day?

5. Fill in the Blank: "Behold, thou knowest what Saul hath done, how he hath cut off those that have familiar spirits, and the _____, out of the land."

Quiz 133
Civil War

1. Whose family fought against David, the newly crowned king of Israel?

2. Where was David ruling at this time?

3. Which powerful soldier switched allegiance because someone asked him an insulting question?

4. True or Trick: David would not meet this powerful soldier unless he brought David's first wife with him.

5. Fill in the Blank: "Deliver me my wife Michal, which I espoused to me for an hundred ____ of the Philistines."

Quiz 134
Abner's Assassination

1. True or Trick: David refused Abner's peace treaty, believing him to be a spy.

2. Where did Joab speak with Abner without David's knowledge?

3. Under which rib did Joab stab Abner?

4. Who was Joab avenging by Abner's death?

5. Fill in the Blank: "And afterward when David heard it, he said, I and my kingdom are ____ before the LORD for ever from the blood of Abner the son of Ner."

Quiz 135
Assassination of a King

1. Which son of Saul followed him as king of Israel?
2. True or Trick: Two of the king's top men beheaded him while he lay on a bed at noon.
3. From whom did the assassins hope to receive a reward?
4. What happened to the assassins?
5. Fill in the Blank: "Shall I not therefore now require his ____ of your hand, and take you away from the earth?"

Quiz 136
David Conquers Jerusalem

1. Before David took over, who inhabited Jerusalem?
2. True or Trick: The inhabitants taunted David and his men, saying that even the blind and the deaf could win against them.
3. How did David and his men enter Jerusalem?
4. How many years did David reign in Jerusalem?
5. Fill in the Blank: "And David went on, and grew ____, and the Lord God of hosts was with him."

Quiz 137
Absalom Murders Amnon

1. How were Absalom and Amnon related?
2. Why was Absalom angry with Amnon?
3. True or Trick: Absalom told his men to kill Amnon when he was drunk.
4. What did everyone else do once they learned of the murder?
5. Fill in the Blank: "Then the king arose, and tare his garments, and lay on the ____; and all his servants stood by with their clothes rent."

Quiz 138
Absalom's Rebellion

1. True or Trick: Absalom stole people's hearts by bribing them with gold.
2. Where did Absalom ask King David for permission to go in order to pay a vow?
3. What was the cue for the people to shout that Absalom reigned?
4. What did David and his men do when they heard of Absalom's revolt?
5. Fill in the Blank: "And Absalom sent for ____ the Gilonite, David's counsellor. . .while he offered sacrifices. And the conspiracy was strong."

Quiz 139
David Leaves Jerusalem

1. True or Trick: The priests wanted the ark of the Lord to go with David, but he said no.

2. Who greeted David and his men with plenty of food?

3. Who threw stones and dust at David and cursed him over and over again?

4. Fill in the Blank: "It may be that the Lord will look on mine ____, and that the Lord will requite me good for his cursing this day."

5. What did Absalom set up on top of the king's house so that he could enjoy David's concubines?

Quiz 140
King Absalom

1. How many men did Ahithophel appoint to pursue David?

2. Who thwarted that idea by suggesting that every man in Israel rise up and fight David?

3. True or Trick: The purpose of the countersuggestion was to give David and his men time to escape.

4. Where did David's messengers hide when Absalom's servants went to kill them?

5. Fill in the Blank: "For the Lord had appointed to defeat the good counsel of Ahithophel, to the intent that the Lord might bring ____ upon Absalom."

Quiz 141
Absalom's Defeat

1. Where did the battle between David's and Absalom's men take place?
2. True or Trick: As Absalom fled on from the battle on horseback, his hair caught on the tree branches and left him dangling.
3. Why didn't the man who came upon Absalom kill him?
4. What did David's army commander Joab do to Absalom?
5. Fill in the Blank: "But this day thou shalt bear no tidings, because the king's son is _____."

Quiz 142
The Lord and Solomon

1. True or Trick: Solomon worshipped the Lord, but he also burned incense in high places.
2. In what city was Solomon when the Lord appeared to him?
3. Name one of three things for which Solomon did *not* ask God.
4. How did God appear to Solomon?
5. Fill in the Blank: "And he came to Jerusalem, and stood before the ark of the covenant of the Lord, and offered up burnt offerings, and offered peace offerings, and made a _____ to all his servants."

Quiz 143
Two Moms, One Baby

1. True or Trick: Two young widows came to Solomon arguing over a live and a dead baby.

2. What did Solomon ask for in order to settle this dispute?

3. What did Solomon propose to do with the live baby?

4. How did the true mother respond?

5. Fill in the Blank: "And all Israel heard of the judgment which the king had judged; and they feared the king: for they saw that the ____ of God was in him, to do judgment."

Quiz 144
The Queen of Sheba

1. How did the queen of Sheba test Solomon's knowledge?

2. What type of animals carried the queen's gifts?

3. True or Trick: The queen of Sheba's main reason for visiting Solomon was to see if all the rumors of his wisdom and wealth were true.

4. What did king Solomon give to her?

5. Fill in the Blank: "Blessed be the LORD thy God, which ____ in thee, to set thee on the throne of Israel."

Quiz 145
The Man with Many Wives

1. How many wives did King Solomon have?
2. How many concubines did King Solomon have?
3. True or Trick: His wives and lovers lured Solomon into worshipping false gods.
4. As punishment for Solomon's disobedience, what did the Lord promise to do?
5. Fill in the Blank: "Of the nations concerning which the LORD said. . . Ye shall not go in to them, neither shall they come in unto you: for surely they will turn away your ____ after their gods."

Quiz 146
A Kingdom Divided

1. Who begged King Rehoboam to lessen the burden and yoke his father Solomon had created?
2. How many days did Rehoboam ask for in order to think the request over?
3. True or Trick: Rehoboam rejected the elders' advice to honor this request and instead followed the young men's advice to increase the hardship.
4. After the kingdom was divided, over what did Rehoboam reign?
5. Fill in the Blank: "So Israel ____ against the house of David unto this day."

Quiz 147
Attempted Reunification

1. How did Rehoboam's taxman Adoram die?
2. True or Trick: Rehoboam decided a civil war would be the best way to reunite the twelve tribes.
3. What other tribe joined Rehoboam and Judah?
4. Who forbade Rehoboam's plan of action?
5. Fill in the Blank: "There was none that followed the house of _____, but the tribe of Judah only."

Quiz 148
Jeroboam's Idolatry

1. What idols did Jeroboam, king of the northern nation of Israel, make for the people to worship?
2. True or Trick: Jeroboam was afraid the people's hearts would become favorable to Jerusalem when they went to sacrifice.
3. What did Jeroboam say his idols had done?
4. Name one of the two cities in which Jeroboam put the idols.
5. Fill in the Blank: "Behold thy _____, O Israel."

Quiz 149
The Man of God and Jeroboam

1. True or Trick: While King Jeroboam burned incense, a man of God pronounced a judgment on the altar itself.

2. What part of Jeroboam dried up when he sought to harm the man of God?

3. What did Jeroboam immediately ask the man of God to do?

4. Who told the man of God he couldn't eat any bread or drink any water while there?

5. Fill in the Blank: "The altar also was rent, and the _____ poured out from the altar, according to the sign which the man of God had given by the word of the LORD."

Quiz 150
Elijah and the Widow

1. What was a certain widow gathering when Elijah met her?

2. What did the widow say she didn't have?

3. True or Trick: After learning how little she had, Elijah told her to first bake something for *him* to eat.

4. How did God provide for the widow?

5. Fill in the Blank: "And she went and did according to the saying of Elijah: and she, and he, and her house, did _____ many days."

Quiz 151
Elijah at Mount Carmel

1. How many of Baal's prophets were there?
2. True or Trick: Elijah's challenge was that the true God would light the bull sacrifice.
3. How long did Baal's prophets cry out to Baal to light their sacrifice?
4. What did Elijah pour over his bull sacrifice to the Lord?
5. Fill in the Blank: "How long halt ye between two ____? If the LORD be God, follow him: but if Baal, then follow him."

Quiz 152
Elijah and God at Horeb

1. True or Trick: Queen Jezebel determined to arrest Elijah and throw him into a dungeon.
2. What did Elijah sit under while in the wilderness hiding from Jezebel?
3. Fill in the Blank: "It is enough; now, O LORD, take away my ____; for I am not better than my fathers."
4. Name one of three things the Lord did not manifest Himself in.
5. True or Trick: The Lord assured Elijah that he was not the last person in Israel who worshipped God.

Quiz 153
Naboth's Vineyard

1. Who wanted Naboth's vineyard?

2. Who took matters into her own hands after Naboth refused to give up the vineyard?

3. True or Trick: Two scoundrels incited the city against Naboth based on lies.

4. How did Naboth die?

5. Fill in the Blank: "Thus saith the LORD, In the place where _____ licked the blood of Naboth shall _____ lick thy blood, even thine." (same word for both blanks)

Quiz 154
Death of a Nasty Queen

1. Who was sent to kill Jezebel?

2. True or Trick: When Jezebel was thrown out a window, her blood splattered on the wall and the horses.

3. What did the executioner do before burying Jezebel?

4. Name one of three things that was left of Jezebel's body.

5. Fill in the Blank: "And the carcase of Jezebel shall be as _____ upon the face of the field in the portion of Jezreel; so that they shall not say, This is Jezebel."

Quiz 155
Miracle of Multiplication

1. Who came to Elisha, asking for help with a huge debt?
2. True or Trick: The creditor threatened to take both daughters from the debtor and make them slaves.
3. What did Elisha tell the debtor to borrow from neighbors?
4. What liquid was multiplied?
5. Fill in the Blank: "And he said, Go, sell the oil, and pay thy debt, and _____ thou and thy children of the rest."

Quiz 156
Poisoned Food

1. What was Elisha's servant originally gathering out in the field for food?
2. What did the servant pick from a vine instead?
3. True or Trick: As everyone started eating, they cried out that there was "death" in the food.
4. What did Elisha use to counter the poison?
5. Fill in the Blank: "And he said, Pour out for the people, that they may eat. And there was no harm in the _____."

Quiz 157
Multiplied Bread Loaves

1. What type of bread did a man bring to Elisha as his firstfruits?
2. How many loaves did the man have?
3. How many men needed to be fed?
4. True or Trick: Elisha touched his staff to the loaves to multiply them.
5. Fill in the Blank: "So he set it before them, and they did ____, and left thereof, according to the word of the LORD."

Quiz 158
Naaman and the King of Israel

1. What disease did the Syrian commander Naaman have?
2. Who suggested that Naaman go to Samaria to be cured?
3. True or Trick: Naaman's king sent a letter to the king of Israel, asking him to heal Naaman.
4. How did the king of Israel respond to the Syrian king's letter?
5. Fill in the Blank: "Am I ____, to kill and to make alive, that this man doth send unto me to recover a man of his leprosy?"

Quiz 159
Naaman and Elisha

1. In what river was Naaman to wash?

2. How many times was Naaman to wash?

3. True or Trick: Naaman was so angry at the perceived disrespect from Elisha that he refused to wash in the river.

4. How was Naaman's skin after his miraculous healing?

5. Fill in the Blank: "Behold, now I know that there is no God in all the earth, but in ____."

Quiz 160
Naaman and Gehazi

1. Who was Gehazi to Elisha?

2. True or Trick: Gehazi lied to Naaman, saying Elisha had guests and needed some silver and clothes from Naaman.

3. Where did Gehazi hide Naaman's gifts before facing Elisha?

4. What was Gehazi's punishment?

5. Fill in the Blank: "And [Elisha] said unto him, Went not mine ____ with thee, when the man turned again from his chariot to meet thee?"

Quiz 161
A Floating Axe Head

1. Into what body of water did the axe head fall?
2. Why was this man so concerned about the axe head?
3. True or Trick: Elisha told the man to fast and pray for three days before the Lord would answer his prayers.
4. What were the men doing beside the water?
5. Fill in the Blank: "And the man of God said, Where fell it? And he shewed him the place. And he cut down a stick, and cast it in thither; and the ____ did swim."

Quiz 162
Fiery Army

1. True or Trick: Although many miles away, Elisha knew every battle plan the Syrian king said in private to his men.
2. What city was Elisha in?
3. What surprise did the enemy king have for Elisha's city one morning?
4. When Elisha's servant's eyes were opened, what were the surrounding hills filled with?
5. Fill in the Blank: "And he answered, Fear not: for they that be with us are ____ than they that be with them."

Quiz 163
Blind Army

1. Who asked God to strike the enemy's army with blindness?
2. True or Trick: The blind army was led straight to the king of Israel before having their vision restored.
3. What did the king of Israel give the enemy army?
4. How did the enemy army respond to the Israelites' treatment?
5. Fill in the Blank: "And [Elisha] answered, Thou shalt not smite them: wouldst thou smite those whom thou hast taken _____ with thy sword and with thy bow?"

Quiz 164
Horrific Famine in Samaria

1. For how many pieces of silver did a tiny amount of dove dung sell during this famine?
2. True or Trick: One woman begged the king of Israel to force another woman to boil her son for food because that's what they'd done to the first woman's son already.
3. What did the king wear under his robes?
4. Who did the king of Israel blame for the famine?
5. Fill in the Blank: "And [the king] said, If the _____ do not help thee, whence shall I help thee? out of the barnfloor, or out of the winepress?"

Quiz 165
The Famine Breaks

1. Who was first to discover a huge stash of necessary food?
2. Where was the food found?
3. What other valuables were discovered along with the food?
4. Where were the owners of the food and valuables?
5. Fill in the Blank: "Then [those who discovered the loot] said to one another, We do not well: this day is a day of good tidings, and we hold our ____."

Quiz 166
King Ahaziah

1. How was King Ahaziah seriously injured?
2. To whom did the king turn for help and answers?
3. What hairy man proclaimed the Lord's judgment toward Ahaziah?
4. True or Trick: When the king repented, God turned His judgment into answered prayer.
5. Fill in the Blank: "Therefore thou shalt not come down off that ____ on which thou art gone up, but shall surely die."

Quiz 167
Athaliah

1. True or Trick: Athaliah appointed herself as queen after her son, the king, was killed.
2. Which of the true king's sons was rescued from the slaughter?
3. Where was this boy hidden?
4. How many years did Athaliah reign?
5. Fill in the Blank: "But Jehoshabeath. . .stole him from among the king's sons that were slain, and put him and his _____ in a bedchamber."

Quiz 168
Young Joash

1. True or Trick: Jehoiada the priest couldn't convince Judah's elders to recognize the young boy as true heir to the throne.
2. Who was to escort the young king to his coronation?
3. Whose weapons did Jehoiada give to the escorts?
4. What two things were given to Joash as he became king?
5. Fill in the Blank: "And Jehoiada and his sons anointed him, and said God _____ the king."

Quiz 169
Ousting the Queen

1. What word did queen Athaliah say twice upon seeing young Joash crowned king?
2. Where was the one place Athaliah was not to be slain?
3. True or Trick: After the people saw the queen was dead, they hurried to protect the house of Baal and his graven images.
4. Who died before the altars of Baal?
5. Fill in the Blank: "And all the people of the land _____ and the city was quiet; after that they had slain Athaliah with the sword.

Quiz 170
Zechariah the Priest

1. True or Trick: Judah's king ordered Zechariah beheaded because he preached God's judgment against the people's false gods.
2. What spiritual leader died, causing the people to forget the Lord?
3. Who forgot the kindness that the late spiritual leader had done for him?
4. How did the one responsible for Zechariah's death end up dying himself?
5. Fill in the Blank: "Thus saith God. . .because ye have _____ the LORD, he hath also _____ you." (same word for both blanks)

Quiz 171
Psalm 23

1. Who is the shepherd of the Shepherd Psalm?
2. True or Trick: God promises to spread a table in the presence of friends.
3. Name one of the two items that comfort the psalmist.
4. Fill in the Blank: "He maketh me to lie down in green ____: he leadeth me beside the still waters."
5. What does the psalmist plan to do in the house of the Lord forever?

Quiz 172
Psalm 51

1. When we do wrong, against whom are we sinning?
2. True or Trick: People are sinners from conception.
3. With what does the psalmist ask God to purge him?
4. Name one of two things that are acceptable sacrifices to God.
5. Fill in the Blank: "Create in me a clean ____, O God; and renew a right spirit within me."

Quiz 173
Psalm 139

1. What two things did David say God had done with him?
2. True or Trick: God knew David before he was even born.
3. What did David say exceeded the number of all the grains of sand in the world?
4. Fill in the Blank: "I will ____ thee, for I am fearfully and wonderfully made."
5. What shines as the day to God?

Quiz 174
Proverbs 31

1. Name one of two qualities that clothe a virtuous woman.
2. Who will rise up and call the Proverbs 31 woman blessed?
3. Fill in the Blank: "Favour is deceitful, and ____ is vain: but a woman that feareth the Lord, she shall be praised."
4. Who does this woman stretch out her hands to help?
5. True or Trick: The Proverbs 31 woman makes sure to get uninterrupted sleep in the nighttime.

Quiz 175
Isaiah 6

1. What king had just died as this chapter unfolded?

2. How many wings did the seraphim have?

3. True or Trick: One of the seraphim took a live coal and touched Isaiah's eyes so that he could see sin the way God does.

4. When God asked who He should send, what did Isaiah answer?

5. Fill in the Blank: "And one cried unto another, and said, Holy, holy, holy, is the Lord of hosts: the whole _____ is full of his glory."

Quiz 176
The Suffering Servant (Isaiah 53)

1. When we sin, what straying animal do we resemble?

2. True or Trick: Although condemned as a criminal, the suffering servant was buried with the rich when he died.

3. What was the purpose of the servant's death?

4. Fill in the Blank: "But he was wounded for our transgressions, he was bruised for our iniquities: the chastisement of our peace was upon him; and with his _____ we are healed."

5. Who was pleased to bruise the suffering servant?

Quiz 177
Dry Bones

1. What place was full of dry bones?
2. True or Trick: Jeremiah watched the bones literally shake and come together into bodies.
3. From how many winds did the life-giving breath come?
4. Once each man was on his feet, what stood in the valley?
5. Fill in the Blank: "And shall put my _____ in you, and ye shall live."

Quiz 178
False Worship in Jerusalem

1. Where was Ezekiel sitting when God took him in spirit to Jerusalem?
2. True or Trick: Ezekiel saw every wicked abomination portrayed on the walls of the Lord's house.
3. What did the false worshippers think God couldn't do?
4. What were the women doing by the gate of the Lord's house?
5. Fill in the Blank: "He said also unto me, Turn thee yet again, and thou shalt see greater _____ that they do."

Quiz 179
The Runaway Prophet

1. To what city was Jonah supposed to travel?
2. To what city did Jonah decide he was going to travel instead?
3. True or Trick: When the huge storm came and the sailors learned it Jonah's fault, they were happy to throw Jonah overboard.
4. What did the sea do as soon as Jonah was tossed overboard?
5. Fill in the Blank: "Then the men _____ the Lord exceedingly, and offered a sacrifice unto the Lord, and made vows."

Quiz 180
The Fishy Prophet

1. How many days was Jonah inside the great fish?
2. What did Jonah do while in the fish's belly?
3. What did the fish eventually do to Jonah?
4. True or Trick: Jonah only had to swim a mile to the shore.
5. Fill in the Blank: "When my soul fainted within me I _____ the Lord: and my prayer came in unto thee, into thine holy temple."

Quiz 181
The Obedient Prophet

1. How many days did Nineveh have before God would carry out His judgment?
2. True or Trick: At first, Nineveh laughed at Jonah, bragging that their gods were more powerful than the Lord.
3. What did Nineveh's king do?
4. Who was exempt from the fast of food and water?
5. Fill in the Blank: "Who can tell if God will turn and repent, and turn away from his fierce _____, that we perish not?"

Quiz 182
The Angry Prophet

1. True or Trick: Jonah was angry with God because God showed mercy to those who didn't deserve it.
2. Why did Jonah sit on the east side of the city?
3. What did God create to give Jonah shade?
4. What destroyed Jonah's shade?
5. Fill in the Blank: "And should not I _____ Nineveh, that great city?"

Quiz 183
Young Daniel

1. What was Daniel's Babylonian name?
2. To which tribe did Daniel and his three friends belong?
3. True or Trick: All the good-looking, intelligent young captives were given three years to learn the Chaldean language and knowledge.
4. How many days did Daniel and his three friends ask to be tested by not eating the king's meat or wine?
5. Fill in the Blank: "As for these four children, God gave them _____ and skill in all learning and wisdom."

Quiz 184
Nebuchadnezzar's First Recorded Dream

1. In what year of Nebuchadnezzar's reign did he have the troubling dream?
2. True or Trick: The king refused to tell anyone his dream, yet demanded his wise men interpret it.
3. What was the first thing Daniel and his three friends did?
4. Name one of the two materials which made up the image's feet in the king's dream.
5. Fill in the Blank: "But there is a God in heaven that revealeth _____, and maketh known to the king Nebuchadnezzar what shall be in the latter days."

Quiz 185
Blazing Fire

1. Of what material was Nebuchadnezzar's extremely tall statue made?

2. Name one of the three men who refused to bow.

3. True or Trick: Nebuchadnezzar called these men and gave them a second chance to bow.

4. How many people did the king see alive and walking around in the fire?

5. Fill in the Blank: "If it be so, our God whom we serve is able to deliver us from the burning fiery ____, and he will deliver us out of thine hand, O king."

Quiz 186
Den of Lions

1. What was the "crime" that landed Daniel in the lions' den as punishment?

2. True or Trick: The king felt bad for Daniel and went home to fast, but he eventually fell asleep.

3. Whom did God send to close the lions' mouths for the entire night?

4. What did the king decree would happen to the men and their families who'd tricked him into signing the law?

5. Fill in the Blank: "So Daniel was taken up out of the den, and no manner of hurt was found upon him, because he ____ in his God."

Quiz 187
Daniel's First Recorded Dream

1. How many beasts were in Daniel's dream?
2. How many heads did the leopard beast have?
3. True or Trick: The bear beast carried an eagle in its mouth.
4. What material made up the fourth beast's teeth?
5. Fill in the Blank: "I beheld till the thrones were cast down, and the _____ of days did sit."

Quiz 188
Queen Vashti

1. In what city did Vashti live?
2. What did the king command Vashti to do?
3. Fill in the Blank: ". . .to shew the people and the princes her beauty: for she was _____ to look on"
4. True or Trick: Vashti refused at first, but under the threat of death, she hurried to obey the king.
5. Whom did the king hope to teach a lesson by taking away Vashti's royal privileges?

Quiz 189
Queen Esther

1. What was Esther's Hebrew name?
2. What relation was Esther to Mordecai, the man who raised her?
3. What was the one thing Mordecai commanded Esther not to do?
4. True or Trick: After twelve months of purification, Esther had to wait three months before seeing the king.
5. Fill in the Blank: "And the king loved Esther above all the women, and she obtained _____ and favour in his sight."

Quiz 190
Mordecai

1. Where was Mordecai sitting when he overheard palace intrigue?
2. True or Trick: Three of the king's guards were so angry with the king, they plotted to kill him.
3. What was the fate of the would-be assassins?
4. How was this incident recorded?
5. Fill in the Blank: "And the thing was known to Mordecai, who _____ it unto Esther the queen."

Quiz 191
Haman

1. Why did Haman plan to kill all the Jewish people in the entire kingdom?

2. How did Haman decide which day to carry out his evil plan?

3. True or Trick: When Mordecai told Esther she had to ask for the king's help, she at first said she couldn't.

4. Why was Haman ordered to publicly honor Mordecai?

5. Fill in the Blank: "And who knoweth whether thou art come to the kingdom for such a ____ as this?"

Quiz 192
Purim

1. How many times did Esther prepare a banquet for the king and Haman before revealing Haman's evil intent?

2. True or Trick: Haman was hanged on the gallows he'd made to hang Mordecai on.

3. How did the king spare the Jewish people from annihilation?

4. How were the Jewish people to remember this victory?

5. Fill in the Blank: "For ____ the Jew was next unto king Ahasuerus, and great among the Jews."

Quiz 193
Nehemiah

1. What was Nehemiah's job?
2. In what city did Nehemiah serve?
3. True or Trick: When Nehemiah heard that Jerusalem's broken walls and burned down gates were still not repaired, he sat down and wept.
4. What did Nehemiah do while he prayed to God?
5. Fill in the Blank: "Let thine ear now be _____, and thine eyes open, that thou mayest hear the prayer of thy servant."

Quiz 194
Nehemiah and the King

1. What did the king see on Nehemiah's face?
2. What did Nehemiah do before making his request to the king?
3. True or Trick: Nehemiah requested a large sum of money be sent to Judah for repairs.
4. Why did Nehemiah ask the king to send a letter to Asaph, the keeper of the king's forest?
5. Fill in the Blank: "And the king granted me, according to the good _____ of my God upon me."

Quiz 195
Nehemiah in Jerusalem

1. How many days did Nehemiah wait before acting?

2. When did Nehemiah inspect the damaged walls and gates?

3. True or Trick: Nehemiah told the priests he was inspecting damage in the city.

4. Which part of the city was so destroyed that Nehemiah's animal couldn't pass?

5. Fill in the Blank: "And they said, Let us rise up and _____. So they strengthened their hands for this good work."

Quiz 196
Nehemiah and the Troublemakers

1. Name one of the ringleaders who tried to stop Nehemiah's repairs.

2. True or Trick: Because of their enemies' threats, Nehemiah and the Jews used one hand to build the walls and the other hand to hold a weapon.

3. After four attempts at tricking Nehemiah into a meeting, what did the enemy bring in his hand in hopes of forcing Nehemiah to stop the rebuilding?

4. How long did it take to finish rebuilding the walls?

5. Fill in the Blank: "The heathen. . .were much cast down in their own eyes: for they perceived that this work was _____ of our God."

Quiz 197
Rebuilding the Temple

1. What Persian king had allowed the Babylonian captives to return to Israel?

2. True or Trick: When the Jews' adversaries heard that the temple was being rebuilt, they offered to help.

3. Name one of the two leaders of Israel who rejected the adversaries' false offer.

4. The enemies' delaying tactics lasted until the installation of what new Persian king?

5. Fill in the Blank: "Then the people of the land ____ the hands of the people of Judah, and troubled them in building."

Quiz 198
Temple Delays

1. What did the adversaries claim the Jews would do if Jerusalem were rebuilt?

2. Which king received a letter from the Jews' enemies such as Bishlam, Mithredath, and Tabeel?

3. True or Trick: After reading the enemies' letter and researching the accusation, the king gave the Jews his blessing to continue anyway.

4. What did the new king, Darius, find that allowed the Jews to continue their work?

5. Fill in the Blank: "Then Tatnai, ____ on this side the river. . .according to that which Darius the king had sent, so they did speedily."

Quiz 199
Finishing the Temple

1. Name one of the two prophets God sent to urge the people to complete the temple's reconstruction.

2. What were the people doing while allowing the Lord's temple to lie in ruins?

3. True or Trick: God cursed the people's neglect by making them work more only to receive less.

4. How did people respond to Haggai's message?

5. Fill in the Blank: "Go up to the mountain, and bring ____, and build the house; and I will take pleasure in it, and I will be glorified, saith the Lord."

Quiz 200
Ezra Prepares to Return

1. To seek God's will, what did Ezra proclaim before heading back to Jerusalem?

2. For what was Ezra too ashamed to ask the king?

3. True or Trick: Ezra explained to the king that God helps those who seek Him but shows wrath to those who forsake Him.

4. In addition to silver and gold, what did the priests and Levites carry back to the temple?

5. Fill in the Blank: "And the hand of our God was upon us, and he ____ us from the hand of the enemy, and of such as lay in wait by the way."

Quiz 201
End of the Old Testament

1. How did Malachi describe the word of the Lord that he carried to Israel?
2. Why was God angry with His people's sacrifices?
3. What group of people had "corrupted the covenant of Levi"?
4. True or Trick: God became weary with the Israelites' belief that "every one that doeth evil is good in the sight of the Lord."
5. Fill in the Blank: "Unto you that fear my name shall the ____ of righteousness arise with healing in his wings."

Quiz 202
Mary's Angelic Visitor

1. How far along was Mary's relative Elizabeth's pregnancy when the angel visited Mary?
2. What was the angel's name?
3. True or Trick: Mary was hesitant at first, explaining that she couldn't possibly be pregnant because she'd kept herself pure according to the Law.
4. What did the angel do after hearing Mary's reply?
5. Fill in the Blank: "For with God ____ shall be impossible."

Quiz 203
Joseph's Fiancée

1. True or Trick: Joseph was already engaged to Mary when he found she was pregnant.
2. What was Joseph prepared to do because he didn't want to make Mary a public example?
3. How did God tell Joseph that Mary's pregnancy was by the Holy Spirit?
4. What does *Emmanuel* mean?
5. Fill in the Blank: "And knew her not till she had brought forth her _____ son: and he called his name Jesus."

Quiz 204
Mary and Elisabeth

1. Where did Mary travel in order to visit Elizabeth?
2. What happened to Elizabeth when she heard Mary's voice?
3. True or Trick: Everyone wanted to name her baby Zacharias, but she insisted on naming him John.
4. How did mute Zacharias communicate his wish for the baby's name?
5. Fill in the Blank: "And blessed is she that _____: for there shall be a performance of those things which were told her from the Lord."

Quiz 205
The First Christmas

1. Who sent out a decree that everyone should be taxed?
2. To whose house and lineage did Joseph belong?
3. True or Trick: Because Mary was carrying the Son of God, Joseph felt it would be safer to avoid staying at an inn.
4. What did Mary use as a crib for Jesus?
5. Fill in the Blank: "And all went to be taxed, every one into his own ____."

Quiz 206
Shepherds Near Bethlehem

1. At what time of day did the shepherds receive the glorious news of Jesus' birth?
2. How many angels delivered the good news?
3. True or Trick: After receiving the good news, the shepherds immediately went to Bethlehem to see what was going on.
4. What did the shepherds do after seeing Jesus?
5. Fill in the Blank: "Glory to God in the highest, and on earth ____, good will toward men."

Quiz 207
Baby Jesus at the Temple

1. True or Trick: Baby Jesus was brought to the temple because every male that opened the womb—the firstborn—was to be called holy to the Lord.

2. Upon seeing baby Jesus, what did Simeon do?

3. Which elderly widow thanked the Lord and prophesied of redemption in Jerusalem?

4. How did Joseph and Mary react to these strangers' proclamations?

5. Fill in the Blank: "For mine eyes have seen thy ____."

Quiz 208
Wise Men

1. From what direction did the wise men travel?

2. What object did the wise men follow?

3. Fill in the Blank: "And when they had opened their ____, they presented unto him gifts; gold, and frankincense, and myrrh."

4. True or Trick: When Herod heard the news of a new king, he was so overjoyed that he ordered a celebration throughout his whole kingdom.

5. What did Herod do with all the children two years old and younger?

Quiz 209
Refugees

1. Fill in the Blank: "Then was fulfilled that which was spoken by ____ the prophet, saying, In Rama was there a voice heard, lamentation, and weeping, and great mourning."
2. To which country did God tell Joseph to take his family and flee?
3. After whose death did God tell Joseph to move his family back to Israel?
4. True or Trick: Because Joseph was afraid of both Archelaus and God's warning, he and his family stayed in Gaza for a while.
5. In what city did Joseph and his family finally settle down?

Quiz 210
Young Jesus at the Temple

1. What occasion brought Jesus and His parents to Jerusalem?
2. How old was Jesus at this time?
3. How far did Mary and Joseph travel toward home before discovering Jesus wasn't with them?
4. True or Trick: Although some were surprised at Jesus' knowledge, the Pharisees dismissed Him because He was just a boy.
5. Fill in the Blank: "And he said unto them, How is it that ye sought me? Wist ye not that I must be about my ____ business?"

Quiz 211
Jesus' Baptism

1. Who baptized Jesus?
2. True or Trick: At first, the one who baptized Jesus claimed he needed to be baptized by Jesus instead.
3. About how old was Jesus when He was baptized?
4. During the baptism, in what form did the Holy Spirit appear?
5. Fill in the Blank: "And there came a ____ from heaven, saying, Thou art my beloved Son, in whom I am well pleased."

Quiz 212
Jesus' Temptations

1. How many days was Jesus tempted in the wilderness?
2. How did Jesus respond to each temptation?
3. True or Trick: The devil quoted scripture to Jesus as part of his temptations.
4. Who led Jesus into the wilderness to be tempted?
5. Fill in the Blank: "And Jesus answering said unto him, It is said, Thou shalt not ____ the Lord thy God."

Quiz 213
Water into Wine

1. What special event formed the backdrop of Jesus' first miracle?
2. Who told Jesus there was no more wine?
3. Fill in the Blank: "His mother saith unto the servants, Whatsoever he saith unto you, _____ it."
4. How many stone water pots were filled with water that Jesus changed into wine?
5. True or Trick: Everyone at the wedding knew Jesus had turned the water into wine.

Quiz 214
The Beatitudes

1. Who will inherit the earth?
2. Fill in the Blank: "Blessed are the _____ in spirit: for theirs is the kingdom of heaven."
3. Who, according to the Beatitudes, will be comforted?
4. True or Trick: Only the perfect in heart will see God.
5. What will happen to those who hunger and thirst after righteousness?

Quiz 215
Requests in the Lord's Prayer

1. What should be done on earth as it is in heaven?
2. For what should we ask each day?
3. True or Trick: We should ask for more forgiveness so that we can show more forgiveness to others.
4. What should we ask God to not lead us into?
5. Fill in the Blank: "But deliver us from ____: For thine is the kingdom, and the power, and the glory, for ever. Amen."

Quiz 216
Matthew

1. What was Matthew's other name?
2. What occupation did Matthew have before becoming Jesus' disciple?
3. True or Trick: Matthew had two questions before he agreed to follow Jesus.
4. When Jesus attended a dinner at Matthew's home, who complained that He was eating with sinners?
5. Fill in the Blank: "I came not to call the righteous, but ____ to repentance."

Quiz 217
Paralytic on the Roof

1. How many men carried a paralytic friend on a mat?

2. How did the friends get the paralytic to Jesus?

3. Fill in the Blank: "When Jesus saw their _____, he said unto the sick of the palsy, Son, thy sins be forgiven thee."

4. True or Trick: The scribes told Jesus He was speaking blasphemies because only God can forgive sins.

5. Why did Jesus heal the paralytic?

Quiz 218
A Woman with a Lengthy Illness

1. How many years did this woman live with an issue of the blood?

2. True or Trick: The woman had spent her entire life savings on doctors but still couldn't be healed.

3. What part of Jesus' clothes did the woman touch?

4. What did Jesus ask the crowd?

5. Fill in the Blank: "And when the woman saw that she was not hid, she came _____, and falling down before him, she declared. . .how she was healed immediately."

Quiz 219
Stampeding Pigs

1. What was the name of the unclean spirits that spoke to Jesus?

2. Where did the man with the unclean spirits live?

3. True or Trick: The unclean spirits forced themselves into a herd of pigs after exiting the man.

4. How many pigs stampeded down the steep hill and drowned in the sea?

5. Fill in the Blank: "Go ____ to thy friends, and tell them how great things the Lord hath done for thee, and hath had compassion on thee."

Quiz 220
Walking on Water

1. What was Jesus doing as His disciples encountered a powerful storm on the Sea of Galilee?

2. True or Trick: Although Jesus was on land, He saw them being battered by the winds and waves.

3. When they saw Jesus walking on water, what did they think He was?

4. Which disciple asked Jesus to command him to walk to Him on the water?

5. Fill in the Blank: "Then they that were in the ship came and ____ him, saying, Of a truth thou art the Son of God."

Quiz 221
Feeding the Five Thousand

1. Why did Jesus ask Philip where they could buy bread?
2. Who told Jesus about the boy with five loaves and two fish?
3. After everyone ate, how many baskets of food were left over?
4. True or Trick: This miracle is recorded in all four Gospels.
5. Fill in the Blank: "When they were filled, he said unto his disciples, ____ up the fragments that remain, that nothing be lost."

Quiz 222
A Nighttime Interview

1. Who came at night to ask Jesus questions about God, heaven, and eternal life?
2. Fill in the Blank: "For God so loved the world, that he gave his only begotten Son, that whosoever ____ in him should not perish, but have everlasting life."
3. What did Jesus say people have to do in order to enter the kingdom of God?
4. To what Old Testament account did Jesus compare His coming death on the cross?
5. True or Trick: The visitor was a Pharisee.

Quiz 223
Woman at the Well

1. In what country did Jesus meet the woman at the well?
2. True or Trick: The woman started the conversation by asking Jesus for water.
3. Where were the disciples at this time?
4. Fill in the Blank: "Come, see a man, which told me all things I ever did: is not this the ____?"
5. How many days did Jesus stay with this woman's people?

Quiz 224
Healing a Boy

1. How does John describe a desperate father from Capernaum?
2. True or Trick: The man's son was about to die.
3. What was unusual about the way Jesus healed the boy?
4. How much time elapsed between Jesus' words and the son's healing?
5. Fill in the Blank: "Then said Jesus unto him, Except ye see signs and wonders, ye will not ____."

Quiz 225
Healing a Sick Man at Bethesda

1. True or Trick: Sick people at this pool waited for an angel to stir the water so that whoever went in first afterward was healed.

2. How many years had this man been sick?

3. On which day of the week did Jesus heal this man?

4. How many times did Jesus talk with the man before he knew who had healed him?

5. Fill in the Blank: "Behold, thou art made whole: _____ no more, lest a worst thing come unto thee."

Quiz 226
Some of Jesus' "I AM" Statements

1. After feeding the five thousand, what did Jesus say He was?

2. Shortly after the Pharisees caught a woman in adultery, what did Jesus say He was?

3. True or Trick: Right after healing a blind man, Jesus said He was both the door of the sheep and the good shepherd.

4. What did Jesus say He was just before bringing Lazarus back to life?

5. Fill in the Blank: "Jesus saith unto him, I am the way, the _____, and the life: no man cometh unto the Father, but by me."

Quiz 227
The Transfiguration

1. How many disciples witnessed Jesus' transfiguration?
2. Name one of the two men who appeared and talked with Jesus.
3. What color did Jesus' clothes become?
4. Fill in the Blank: "And a voice came out of the cloud, saying, This is my beloved Son: _____ him."
5. True or Trick: As His disciples came down the mountain after the transfiguration, Jesus commanded them to say nothing until after He rose from the dead.

Quiz 228
Mary and Martha

1. Which sister owned the home which Jesus and His disciples visited?
2. Which sister sat at Jesus' feet, listening to Him?
3. True or Trick: One sister was irritated at Jesus for not rebuking the other's laziness.
4. What was the busy sister trying to do?
5. Fill in the Blank: "But one thing is _____: and Mary hath chosen that good part, which shall not be taken away from her."

Quiz 229
Rich Young Ruler

1. What was this man's question to Jesus?
2. Who did Jesus say was the only one who is good?
3. What did Jesus tell the man to do?
4. True or Trick: The man quickly did what Jesus said.
5. Fill in the Blank: "With men this is ____; but with God all things are possible."

Quiz 230
Tax Advice

1. Who joined with the Pharisees in hopes of trapping Jesus with His words?
2. Fill in the Blank: "Is it ____ to give tribute to Caesar, or not?"
3. For what type coin did Jesus ask?
4. Whose image and inscription were on the coin?
5. True or Trick: Jesus said taxes should be paid.

Quiz 231
The Widow's Offering

1. Where was Jesus when He watched people donating their money?
2. How many mites, or coins, did the poor widow give?
3. True or Trick: The rich were misers and donated very little.
4. Fill in the Blank: "For all they did cast in of their ____; but she of her want did cast in all that she had, even all her living."
5. Whom did Jesus call over to teach this lesson?

Quiz 232
Parable of the Wheat and Tares

1. When did an enemy sow tares in a man's wheat fields?
2. Why did the owner forbid his servants from removing the tares while the wheat grew?
3. According to Jesus, what does the field represent?
4. True or Trick: The harvest is the end of the world, and the reapers are the angels.
5. Fill in the Blank: "Then shall the ____ shine forth as the sun in the kingdom of their Father."

Quiz 233
Parable of the Net

1. What did the net represent?

2. When was the net drawn to the shore?

3. Who will divide the wicked from the just?

4. True or Trick: The net was cast into the river and gathered all kinds of fish.

5. Fill in the Blank: "And shall cast them into the _____ of fire: there will be wailing and gnashing of teeth."

Quiz 234
Parable of the Sower

1. How many places did the sower's seed fall?

2. What does the seed represent?

3. Fill in the Blank: "But that on the good ground are they, which in an honest and good heart, having heard the word, _____ it, and bring forth fruit with patience."

4. True or Trick: The first batch of seeds fell on the path, only to be eaten by wild beasts.

5. What did the thorns do to the seeds?

Quiz 235
Parable of the Good Samaritan

1. To what city was a man traveling when the thieves beat him up and left him half dead?
2. Name one of the two people who passed by this man without helping him.
3. True or Trick: The Samaritan bandaged the man's wounds, put him on his own beast, and took him to his home and family.
4. What did the Samaritan promise the innkeeper?
5. Fill in the Blank: "Then said Jesus unto him, Go, and do thou _____."

Quiz 236
Parable of the Vineyard Owner

1. Name one of the two structures in the vineyard.
2. Where was the vineyard owner during the growing season and harvest?
3. True or Trick: The entrusted husbandmen beat up, stoned, and killed the owner's servants who came to collect the vineyard's fruits.
4. In a last-ditch effort, whom did the owner send to the tenants?
5. Fill in the Blank: "Therefore say I unto you, The kingdom of God shall be _____ from you, and given to a nation bringing forth the fruits thereof."

Quiz 237
Parable of the Virgins

1. What person were the virgins waiting to meet?
2. How many virgins were wise?
3. At what time did the special visitor finally arrive?
4. True or Trick: After the foolish virgins bought oil and came back, they had to wait three days before being allowed in.
5. Fill in the Blank: "But he answered and said, Verily I say to you, I know you ____."

Quiz 238
Parable of the Talents

1. How many talents did the first servant receive?
2. True or Trick: The servant with the one talent dug a hole and buried it for safekeeping.
3. When it came time to settle accounts, how many new talents had the second servant earned?
4. With which servant was the lord angry?
5. Fill in the Blank: "But from him that hath not shall be taken ____ even that which he hath."

Quiz 239
Parable of the Wedding Banquet

1. In the parable, what did the king represent?
2. How many of the original invited guests actually came to the banquet?
3. True or Trick: The king invited people on the highways, both good and bad.
4. What happened to the man who wasn't wearing a wedding garment?
5. Fill in the Blank: "For many are called, but few are ____."

Quiz 240
Parable of the Lost Sheep

1. How many sheep were *not* lost?
2. True or Trick: Although the shepherd was relieved to have his sheep back, he punished it by separating it from the flock for three days.
3. How did the shepherd carry the lost sheep?
4. What did the shepherd do as soon as he got home?
5. Fill in the Blank: "____ with me; for I have found my sheep which was lost."

Quiz 241
Parable of the Lost Coin

1. How many coins were not lost?
2. Of what material was the coin made?
3. True or Trick: The woman lit a candle and swept the house in hopes of finding her lost coin.
4. What did the woman do when she finally found the coin?
5. Fill in the Blank: "Likewise, I say unto you, there is _____ in the presence of the angels of God over one sinner that repenteth."

Quiz 242
A Woman Who Couldn't Straighten Up

1. How many years was this woman bent over?
2. On what day of the week did Jesus heal this woman?
3. True or Trick: The ruler of the synagogue was happy Jesus had healed this woman.
4. What "work" did Jesus say His audience did, regardless of the day?
5. Fill in the Blank: "And when he had said these things, all his adversaries were ashamed: and all the people _____."

Quiz 243
Jesus Heals Lepers

1. How many lepers begged Jesus for healing?
2. True or Trick: Jesus healed them while they went to show themselves to the priests.
3. How many lepers didn't come back to thank Jesus?
4. What nationality was the non-Jewish leper?
5. Fill in the Blank: "Arise, go thy way: thy ____ hath made thee whole."

Quiz 244
Blind Bartimaeus

1. How did the crowd react to Bartimaeus' cries for mercy?
2. How did Jesus react?
3. What city was the setting for this story?
4. True or Trick: Jesus made a mixture of spit and mud, put it on the man's eyes, and told him to wash it off at Bethesda's pool.
5. Fill in the Blank: "And all the people, when they saw it, gave ____ unto God."

Quiz 245
Zaccheaus

1. Why did Zacchaeus climb up a tree?
2. What type of tree was it?
3. True or Trick: Jesus invited himself to Zacchaeus' house.
4. How did Zacchaeus receive Jesus?
5. Fill in the Blank: "And Jesus said unto him, This day is _____ come to this house, forsomuch as he also is a son of Abraham."

Quiz 246
The Anointing at Bethany

1. How much costly spikenard did Mary pour over Jesus' feet?
2. What did Mary wipe Jesus' feet with?
3. Which disciple was angered by this "waste"?
4. True or Trick: This disciple was actually angry because he was a thief who'd hoped to steal the profits.
5. Fill in the Blank: "Then said Jesus, Let her alone: against the day of my _____ hath she kept this."

Quiz 247
Palm Sunday

1. How many disciples did Jesus send to find a young donkey?

2. How many donkeys were they supposed to bring back to Jesus?

3. True or Trick: If anyone asked questions, the disciples were to say, "The Lord will reward you if you lend the donkey to Him."

4. Why were there large crowds of people already at Jerusalem?

5. Fill in the Blank: "I tell you that if these should hold their peace, the _____ would immediately cry out."

Quiz 248
Foot Washing

1. Name one of the two items Jesus used when He washed His disciples' feet.

2. Which disciple refused to let Jesus wash his feet at first?

3. True or Trick: Jesus washed Judas Iscariot's feet as well, even though Jesus knew the devil already had convinced Judas to betray Him.

4. Why did Jesus wash the disciples' feet?

5. Fill in the Blank: "The _____ is not greater than his lord; neither he that is sent greater than he that sent him."

Quiz 249
A Plot to Kill Jesus

1. Besides Jesus, whom else did the chief priests want to murder?

2. How many pieces of silver did Judas receive as payment for betraying Jesus?

3. Fill in the Blank: "And he cast down the pieces of silver in the temple, and departed, and went and ____ himself."

4. True or Trick: Since the chief priests couldn't put Judas' returned silver in the temple treasury, they bought a shepherd's field to bury strangers in.

5. Who said it was better that one man die for the people instead of the whole nation?

Quiz 250
Peter Denies Jesus

1. True or Trick: Peter was allowed into the temple courtyard because he was with another disciple whom the high priest knew.

2. How many times did Peter deny knowing Jesus?

3. What animal made a sound just after Peter's final denial?

4. How many times did this animal make a sound?

5. Fill in the Blank: "And Peter went out, and wept ____."

Quiz 251
Jesus vs. the Sanhedrin

1. True or Trick: No one was able to find a reason, true or false, to execute Jesus.

2. What was wrong with all of the testimony against Jesus?

3. After blindfolding Jesus, what did the men who held Him keep doing?

4. To whom was Jesus brought before He faced the high priest Caiaphas?

5. Fill in the Blank: "What think ye? They answered and said, He is _____ of death."

Quiz 252
Jesus Arrested

1. How did Judas let the armed mob and soldiers identify Jesus?

2. What did the crowd do the first time Jesus answered, "I am he"?

3. True or Trick: A young man, wearing only a linen cloth, was watching the proceedings, and when the crowd grabbed him, he left the cloth behind and ran away naked.

4. What was the name of the high priest's servant, whose ear Peter cut off?

5. Fill in the Blank: "But how then shall the scriptures be _____, that thus it must be?"

Quiz 253
Jesus before Herod

1. Who sent Jesus to be tried by Herod?
2. True or Trick: Herod regarded Jesus like a performer, wanting Him to do a miracle or two for Herod's pleasure.
3. How did Jesus answer every one of Herod's questions?
4. Who became Herod's good friend after this event?
5. Fill in the Blank: "And when Herod saw Jesus, he was exceeding ____."

Quiz 254
Jesus or Barabbas

1. Name one of the crimes Barabbas had committed.
2. True or Trick: While Pilate sat on the judgment seat, his son warned him to have nothing to do with Jesus.
3. What prompted this warning to Pilate?
4. Who stirred up the crowd to ask for Barabbas and destroy Jesus?
5. Fill in the Blank: "And so Pilate, willing to ____ the people, released Barabbas unto them."

Quiz 255
Soldiers Mock Jesus

1. In what color robe did the soldiers dress Jesus as part of their mockery?
2. What did the soldiers use to make a crude crown for Jesus?
3. What did the soldiers use to make a crude scepter?
4. True or Trick: The soldiers spit on Jesus, hit Him, and mockingly bowed before Him.
5. Fill in the Blank: "And after that they had mocked him, they took the robe off from him, and put his own raiment on him, and led him away to _____ him."

Quiz 256
Crucified

1. What was the homeland of Simon, who was compelled to carry Jesus' cross for Him?
2. What besides Golgotha was Jesus' crucifixion site called?
3. What was mixed with wine and offered to Jesus on the cross?
4. True or Trick: Jesus' garments were given to the soldier who did the crucifying.
5. Fill in the Blank: "And the superscription of his _____ was written over, THE KING OF THE JEWS."

Quiz 257
Two Criminals

1. True or Trick: At first, both criminals joined the crowd in mocking Jesus.
2. What did the first criminal demand of Jesus?
3. How did the second criminal respond to the first criminal?
4. What did the second criminal ask of Jesus?
5. Fill in the Blank: "And Jesus said unto him, Verily I say unto thee, Today shalt thou be with me in ____."

Quiz 258
Jesus' Death

1. What did Jesus' cry *"Eli, Eli, lama sabachthani"* translate to?
2. What happened to the temple curtain as Jesus died?
3. True or Trick: An earthquake happened, graves opened, and many dead saints arose from the dead when Jesus died.
4. Who did the centurion think was crucified on the cross?
5. Fill in the Blank: "When Jesus therefore had received the vinegar, he said, It is ____: and he bowed his head, and gave up the ghost."

Quiz 259
Jesus' Burial

1. Who was surprised to learn that Jesus was already dead, summoning a centurion to confirm the news?
2. Name one of two liquids that flowed from Jesus' dead body when a soldier pierced His side.
3. Name one of two people who made sure Jesus had a proper burial.
4. True or Trick: Jesus was buried in a tomb with one other dead person—a young boy.
5. Fill in the Blank: "And he rolled a great _____ to the door of the sepulchre, and departed."

Quiz 260
Jesus' Resurrection

1. At what time of the day did Mary Magdalene find the tomb empty?
2. True or Trick: On resurrection morning, the angel of the Lord came down from heaven, rolled back the stone, and sat on it, causing a massive earthquake.
3. Along with Peter, who ran to the tomb upon hearing the good news?
4. What did no one see in the tomb?
5. Fill in the Blank: "Why seek ye the _____ among the dead? He is not here, but is risen."

Quiz 261
Soldiers Guarding the Tomb

1. Name one of two groups of people who came to Pilate asking that the tomb be secured and watched by Roman soldiers.
2. True or Trick: The Jewish leaders wanted to make sure the disciples didn't steal the body in apparent fulfillment of Jesus' prophecy of resurrection.
3. On Easter morning, to whom did the soldiers report regarding the empty tomb?
4. What did the soldiers receive in return for spreading the lie that the disciples stole the body at night while they slept?
5. Fill in the Blank: "And this _____ is commonly reported among the Jews until this day."

Quiz 262
Jesus Appears to Mary Magdalene

1. Upon seeing the stone rolled away and the tomb empty, what did Mary Magdalene do?
2. What was Mary doing outside Jesus' tomb?
3. True or Trick: When Mary first saw Jesus, she thought He was a priest coming to check on the tomb.
4. What did Jesus tell Mary *not* to do since He had not yet ascended to His Father?
5. Fill in the Blank: "Jesus saith unto her, Mary. She turned herself, and saith unto him, Rabboni; which is to say, _____."

Quiz 263
Doubting Thomas

1. Why did Thomas doubt that Jesus rose from the dead?

2. Name one of two things Thomas said he'd have to do before he believed Jesus was alive again.

3. True or Trick: Thomas had to wait three days before he saw Jesus.

4. What did Thomas say to Jesus when he finally believed?

5. Fill in the Blank: "Jesus saith unto him, Thomas, because thou hast seen me, thou hast believed: _____ are they that have not seen, and yet have believed."

Quiz 264
On the Road to Emmaus

1. How many of Jesus' followers were walking to Emmaus?

2. True or Trick: At some point on their journey, the risen Jesus joined them, but they didn't recognize Him.

3. What were the disciples discussing?

4. What did Jesus do before their eyes were opened and they understood who He was?

5. Fill in the Blank: "And they said one to another, Did not our _____ burn within us, while he talked with us by the way, and while he opened to us the scriptures?"

Quiz 265
Jesus Serves Breakfast

1. In what sea did the disciples go fishing?
2. True or Trick: For a whole night's effort, all the men caught were three small fish.
3. On which side of the boat did Jesus command the men to let down their nets?
4. How many fish did the disciples then catch?
5. What did Jesus have on the coals when the men reached shore?

Quiz 266
Peter Restored

1. Why was Peter soaked when he came to breakfast?
2. True or Trick: Jesus asked Peter four times if Peter really loved Him.
3. What did Jesus instruct Peter to do for His sheep?
4. True or Trick: Jesus gave Peter a hint of the way he would ultimately die.
5. Fill in the Blank: "And when he had spoken this, he saith unto him, _____ me."

Quiz 267
The Ascension

1. What did Jesus command His disciples *not* to do before receiving His Father's promise?

2. While His disciples watched Jesus ascend, what hid Him from sight?

3. Who appeared after Jesus disappeared?

4. Fill in the Blank: "Ye shall be ____ unto me both in Jerusalem, and in all Judea, and in Samaria, and unto the uttermost part of the earth."

5. True or Trick: Just before Jesus ascended, the disciples asked Him one last time about the future.

Quiz 268
Pentecost

1. What did the coming of the Holy Spirit sound like?

2. What did the coming of the Spirit look like?

3. What unique thing suddenly happened with the disciples' speech?

4. True or Trick: Some of the doubters accused the disciples of being drunk.

5. Fill in the Blank: "And they were all amazed and marvelled, saying one to another, Behold, are not all these which speak ____?"

Quiz 269
The Fatal Lie

1. How were Ananias and Sapphira related to each other?
2. What did the couple lie about?
3. True or Trick: Although they came at separate times, they both fell dead on the spot when confronted with their lie.
4. Who exposed the couple's lie?
5. Fill in the Blank: "Why hast thou _____ this thing in thine heart? thou hast not lied unto men, but unto God."

Quiz 270
Prison Break

1. Who was thrown in prison for preaching the Gospel and healing the sick?
2. Who opened their prison doors at night?
3. Where did the prison officials find the former prisoners the next morning?
4. True or Trick: A Pharisee named Joseph said the Jewish leaders should leave the prisoners alone in case they really were sent by God.
5. Fill in the Blank: "We ought to _____ God rather than men."

Quiz 271
Stephen

1. What were the original duties of Stephen and six fellow church members?

2. What did Stephen do because he was full of faith and power?

3. What was the real reason certain people disputed and hated Stephen?

4. True or Trick: The apostle Paul watched as Stephen was stoned.

5. Fill in the Blank: "But he, being _____ of the Holy Ghost, looked up steadfastly into heaven, and saw the glory of God, and Jesus standing on the right hand of God."

Quiz 272
An Ethiopian Official's Conversion

1. Who told a certain disciple to travel toward Gaza?

2. Which disciple was commissioned to go?

3. Where did the disciple find the Ethiopian official?

4. True or Trick: The Ethiopian read from the prophet Jeremiah but didn't understand what was being said.

5. Fill in the Blank: "And he answered and said, I _____ that Jesus Christ is the Son of God."

Quiz 273
Saul's Dramatic Conversion

1. To what city was Saul heading in order to arrest believers and bring them to Jerusalem?
2. True or Trick: When the Lord appeared to Saul, he both saw a light and heard a voice, but the men with him heard and saw nothing.
3. How many days was Saul without sight?
4. Who did the Lord use to restore Saul's sight?
5. Fill in the Blank: "Go thy way: for he is a _____ vessel unto me, to bear my name before the Gentiles, and kings, and the children of Israel."

Quiz 274
Saul's Escape over the Wall

1. What did the Jews watch day and night in hopes of catching Saul?
2. Who helped Saul escape?
3. In what did Saul escape?
4. True or Trick: When Saul got to Jerusalem, the only person who believed he was really a Christian was Barnabas.
5. Fill in the Blank: "And he spake _____ in the name of the Lord Jesus."

Quiz 275
Dorcas

1. What other name did Dorcas have?
2. What did Dorcas make for needy women?
3. Which apostle kneeled down by the dead Dorcas, prayed, and saw God bring her to life?
4. True or Trick: This story occurred near Ephesus.
5. Fill in the Blank: "And he gave her his hand, and lifted her up, and when he had called the saints and widows, presented her ____."

Quiz 276
Peter and Cornelius

1. What rank did Cornelius have in the Italian band regiment army?
2. Who appeared and spoke with Cornelius while he prayed one day?
3. True or Trick: In Peter's vision, all manner of unclean animals, bugs, and birds were lowered from above on a sheet.
4. How many times did the vision recur to Peter?
5. Fill in the Blank: "But God hath shewed me that I should not call any man common or ____."

Quiz 277
Apostolic Prison Break

1. True or Trick: On the night before his scheduled execution, Paul was in prison, bound with two chains, and sleeping between two guards.

2. What did the angel of the Lord do to rouse the sleeping apostle?

3. What did the apostle think was happening?

4. What servant girl was so excited by the apostle's knocking at the gate that she forgot to let him in?

5. Fill in the Blank: "And they said unto her, Thou art mad. But she constantly affirmed that it was even so. Then said they, It is his ____."

Quiz 278
Herod's Painful Death

1. What was Herod doing with the people of Tyre and Sidon?

2. True or Trick: The audience proclaimed that Herod was a god, not a man.

3. Why was Herod punished?

4. How did Herod die?

5. Fill in the Blank: "But the word of God grew and ____."

Quiz 279
Mission Field Preparations

1. From what city were the first missionaries sent?
2. How many people were being considered for the mission field?
3. Name one of the two people the Holy Ghost picked.
4. True or Trick: Before these two left, everyone took the Lord's Supper.
5. Fill in the Blank: "So they, being sent forth by the Holy Ghost, departed unto Seleucia; and from thence they sailed to ____."

Quiz 280
Mistaken for Gods

1. In what city were Paul and Barnabas mistaken for gods?
2. What miracle caused the people to reach that conclusion?
3. True or Trick: The crowd believed Barnabas was Jupiter and Paul was Mercury.
4. What did Paul and Barnabas do with their clothes?
5. Fill in the Blank: "We also are men of like ____ with you, and preach unto you that ye should turn from these vanities unto the living God."

Quiz 281
Missionary Squabble

1. Who was the subject of Barnabas and Paul's disagreement regarding missionary service?
2. What had this person done to cause the disagreement?
3. True or Trick: The disagreement was so sharp that Paul and Barnabas parted ways.
4. What happened to the person who caused such a ruckus?
5. Fill in the Blank: "And Paul chose _____, and departed, being recommended by the brethren unto the grace of God."

Quiz 282
Timothy Enters the Picture

1. Who decided to involve Timothy on the missionary team?
2. True or Trick: Timothy's dad was Jewish, but his mom was Greek.
3. Name one of the two cities in which the believers spoke highly of Timothy.
4. Why was Timothy circumcised?
5. Fill in the Blank: "And so were the _____ established in the faith, and increased in number daily."

Quiz 283
Lydia

1. True or Trick: Paul met Lydia in the city of Thyatira.
2. What was Lydia's occupation?
3. Where did all the women meet and pray each Sabbath?
4. After she believed and was baptized, what did Lydia ask Paul and his company to do?
5. Fill in the Blank: "Whose ____ the Lord opened, that she attended unto the things which were spoken of Paul."

Quiz 284
Fortune-Telling Slave Girl

1. True or Trick: This girl followed Paul and Silas around town for many days, shouting that they were servants of God who knew the way of salvation.
2. What did Paul do to upset her masters?
3. What did the magistrates do to Paul and Silas?
4. What did the jailer do with the missionaries?
5. Fill in the Blank: "These men, being ____, do exceedingly trouble our city."

Quiz 285
Yet Another Jail Break

1. Name one of the two things Paul and Silas did while stuck in prison at midnight.
2. What loosed the prisoners?
3. True or Trick: Although Paul and Silas stayed, most of the prisoners fled.
4. What ultimately happened with the jailer?
5. Fill in the Blank: "And they said, Believe on the Lord Jesus Christ, and thou shalt be _____, and thy house."

Quiz 286
Corinthian Church Start-Up

1. What prompted Paul to witness exclusively to the Corinthian Gentiles?
2. What was Paul's occupation while in Corinth?
3. True or Trick: Crispus, the chief ruler of the synagogue, and all his house believed on the Lord.
4. How long did Paul stay in Corinth?
5. Fill in the Blank: "Then spake the Lord to Paul in the night by a vision, Be not _____, but speak, and hold not thy peace."

Quiz 287
Riot in Ephesus

1. What silversmith started the trouble in Ephesus?
2. True or Trick: The ringleader convinced the other craftsmen that Paul's teachings threatened their livelihood.
3. What Greek goddess did the people praise?
4. How long did the mob shout in the theater before the town clerk calmed them down?
5. Fill in the Blank: "Seeing then that these things cannot be spoken against, ye ought to be quiet, and to do nothing ____."

Quiz 288
Eutychus' Miracle

1. Where was Eutychus sitting when he fell asleep?
2. At what hour did he fall asleep?
3. True or Trick: Eutychus fell to his death.
4. Who was present to work a miracle?
5. Fill in the Blank: "And they brought the young man ____."

Quiz 289
A Plot to Kill

1. True or Trick: A group of Jewish men made an oath to neither eat nor drink until they had killed young Timothy.

2. How many men were in this conspiracy?

3. Who overheard the men plotting?

4. To whom was this person brought to tell what he'd overheard?

5. Fill in the Blank: "And he called unto him two centurions, saying, Make ready two hundred soldiers to go to ____."

Quiz 290
Paul Shipped to Rome

1. True or Trick: Paul warned the centurion overseeing the ship of impending danger.

2. After how many days of storm did people start throwing the ship's tackle and gear overboard?

3. After how many days in the storm did the ship near land?

4. Who tried to escape the ship and leave everyone else behind?

5. Fill in the Blank: "Wherefore I pray you take some ____: for this is for your health: for there shall not an hair fall from the head of any of you."

Quiz 291
Shipwreck!

1. When the ship ran aground, what happened to its back part?
2. What did the soldiers plan to do with all the prisoners?
3. Who thwarted the soldiers' plan?
4. True or Trick: People either swam to shore or floated there on broken pieces of the ship.
5. Fill in the Blank: "And so it came to pass, that they escaped all ____ to land."

Quiz 292
Island Hospitality

1. True or Trick: The island where Paul and company landed was hot and arid.
2. What came out of the sticks Paul gathered for a fire?
3. What did the islanders assume Paul was being punished for?
4. When Paul didn't die, what did the islanders then assume he was?
5. Fill in the Blank: "And when they were escaped, then they knew that the island was called ____."

Quiz 293
Island Miracle

1. Whose father lay sick with a fever?
2. Fill in the Blank: "To whom Paul entered in, and prayed, and laid his ____ on him, and healed him."
3. True or Trick: After God answered Paul's prayer for healing, the islanders were afraid to anger Paul because they thought he was a powerful god.
4. How long did the shipwrecked people stay on the island?
5. Which two gods served as the figurehead of Paul's new ship?

Quiz 294
Love, or Charity

1. Fill in the Blank: "And though I have all faith, so that I could remove mountains, and have not charity, I am ____."
2. In what does charity rejoice?
3. True or Trick: Although faith, hope, and love are the top three qualities, faith is the greatest of the three.
4. Name one of the four things love always does.
5. What did Paul say charity, or love, *never* does?

Quiz 295
The Whole Armour of God

1. Against what do believers *not* wrestle?
2. True or Trick: Righteousness is represented by a helmet.
3. What does the shield of faith quench?
4. What should we be doing continually in the Spirit?
5. Fill in the Blank: "Wherefore take unto you the whole armour of God, that ye may be able to withstand in the evil day, and having done all, to _____."

Quiz 296
Philemon

1. True or Trick: Philemon was a runaway slave, and Onesimus his owner.
2. In what season of life was Paul when he met the runaway slave?
3. What did Paul command the owner to do?
4. What promise did Paul make to the slave's former owner?
5. Fill in the Blank: "Which in time past was to thee _____, but now profitable to thee and to me."

Quiz 297
Letters to Seven Churches

1. If the church at Ephesus didn't repent and return to their first love, what would it lose?

2. Which church was lukewarm?

3. Fill in the Blank: "He that hath an ear, let him hear what the _____ saith unto the churches."

4. As a reward for faithfulness, which church was given an open door that no one can close?

5. True or Trick: In Pergamos' letter, the victor is promised a new name that no one will know except the person receiving it.

Quiz 298
End Times

1. The order of judgments during the Tribulation begins with seven bowls, followed by seven trumpets, then seven seals.

2. How many years will the dragon be bound and chained in the abyss?

3. Fill in the Blank: "And I will give power unto my two _____, and they shall prophesy a thousand two hundred and threescore days, clothed in sackcloth."

4. At the great white throne of judgment, who will be thrown into the lake of fire last?

5. Who will dwell with everyone living in the New Jerusalem?

Quiz 299
The Great White Throne of Judgment

1. Name one of two things that fled away from God when He sat on the great white throne.
2. True or Trick: God has two types of books: the book of life and the books that contain every deed done by every person.
3. Who will stand before God at judgment?
4. If their names aren't written in the book of life, according to what will people be judged?
5. Fill in the Blank: "And _____ was not found written in the book of life was cast into the lake of fire."

Quiz 300
New Jerusalem

1. True or Trick: Earth and space will one day pass away and be replaced by a new heaven and earth.
2. In John's vision, where did the new Jerusalem come from?
3. How many gates will the new Jerusalem have?
4. With what were the foundations of the new Jerusalem decorated?
5. Fill in the Blank: "Behold, the _____ of God is with men, and he will dwell with them, and they shall be his people, and God himself shall be with them, and be their God."

Answer Key

Quiz 1: **Christmas**

1. Trick. Only Matthew and Luke do (Matthew 1:18–2:23; Luke 1:5–2:40)
2. the angel Gabriel (Luke 1:26–31)
3. shepherds (Luke 2:7–15)
4. Simeon (Luke 2:25–26)
5. gold (Matthew 2:11)

Quiz 2: **Easter**

1. Golgotha (Matthew 27:33)
2. God (Matthew 27:46)
3. True (Mark 15:21)
4. Judas Iscariot (Luke 22:47–48)
5. Mary Magdalene (John 20:1, 11–18)

Quiz 3: **Psalms**

1. 150
2. Psalm 90
3. True (Psalm 31:5 and Luke 23:46)
4. Psalm 88
5. word (Psalm 119:105)

Quiz 4: **Hands and Fingers**

1. written (Exodus 31:18)
2. Pharaoh's magicians (Exodus 8:18–19)
3. six (2 Samuel 21:20)
4. True (John 10:28)
5. on the ground (John 8:6)

Quiz 5: **Salvation**

1. boast (Ephesians 2:8–9)
2. confess aloud the Lord Jesus, believe in one's heart God raised Jesus from the dead (Romans 10:9)
3. True (Titus 3:5)
4. the Father (John 14:6)
5. men (Acts 4:12)

Quiz 6: **Messianic Prophesies**

1. Isaiah (Isaiah 7:14)
2. Micah (Micah 5:2)
3. Zechariah (Zechariah 9:9)
4. Trick. It was Zechariah (Zechariah 11:12–13)
5. bruised (Isaiah 53:5)

Quiz 7: **Fish**

1. the fifth (Genesis 1:20–23)
2. Egypt (Numbers 11:5)
3. True (Jonah 1:17)
4. Simon Peter, Andrew, James, John (Matthew 4:18–19; Mark 1:19)
5. follow (Matthew 4:19)

Quiz 8: **Weirdest Things Eaten**

1. the golden calf idol (Exodus 32:19–20)
2. True (2 Kings 6:25–29)
3. Ezekiel (Ezekiel 2:8–3:2)
4. fruit of the tree of the knowledge of good and evil (Genesis 3:6–7)
5. book (Revelation 10:10)

Quiz 9: **Fun Facts**

1. Psalm 119 (176 verses)
2. Psalm 117 (2 verses)
3. Esther 8:9
4. Trick. John 11:35 is also two words, but fewer letters: "Jesus wept."
5. profitable (2 Timothy 3:16)

Quiz 10: **Riddles and Hard Sayings**

1. Samson (Judges 14:13–14, 18)
2. proverb (Proverbs 1:6)
3. Daniel (Daniel 5:11–12)
4. Trick. He does occasionally (Ezekiel 17:1–10)
5. Moses' faithfulness (Numbers 12:7–8)

Quiz 11: **Famous Murderers**
1. Cain (Genesis 4:8)
2. Trick. It was Moses (Exodus 2:11–12)
3. David (2 Samuel 11:14–17, 26–27)
4. Herod (Matthew 2:16)
5. the king of Egypt (Exodus 1:15–16)

Quiz 12: **Our Adversary's Places of Abode**
1. True (Ezekiel 28:14)
2. the air (Ephesians 2:2)
3. the earth (Revelation 12:9)
4. the bottomless pit (Revelation 20:1–3)
5. lake (Revelation 20:10)

Quiz 13: **Asking and Receiving**
1. delight yourself in the Lord (Psalm 37:4)
2. Jesus (Matthew 7:7, 28)
3. Trick. There must be no wavering (James 1:6–8)
4. selfish ones (James 4:3)
5. name (John 16:23)

Quiz 14: **Herbs and Spices**
1. manna (Exodus 16:31)
2. Gilead (Jeremiah 8:22)
3. linen clothes (John 19:40)
4. True (Matthew 23:23)
5. a mustard seed (Matthew 13:31)

Quiz 15: **God's Voice**
1. Adam and Eve (Genesis 3:8)
2. Samuel (1 Samuel 3:1–10)
3. the Israelites in the wilderness (Deuteronomy 5:22)
4. True (1 Kings 19:12–13)
5. beloved (Matthew 3:17)

Quiz 16: **Cursed by God**

1. the serpent (Genesis 3:13–14)
2. thorns, thistles (Genesis 3:17–19)
3. Trick. He cursed a fig tree (Mark 11:12–14, 20–21)
4. the new heaven and new earth (Revelation 22:1–3)
5. man (Jeremiah 17:5)

Quiz 17: **God's Word**

1. by God's Holy Spirit (2 Peter 1:21)
2. forever (Isaiah 40:8)
3. Trick. Don't even think about doing that! (Deuteronomy 4:2; Revelation 22:18–19)
4. "return. . .void" (Isaiah 55:11)
5. beginning (John 1:1)

Quiz 18: **Cows**

1. Pharaoh (Genesis 41:1–4)
2. Aaron and the Israelites (Exodus 32:1–6)
3. red (Numbers 19:2)
4. Trick. The Philistines did that (1 Samuel 6:1, 7)
5. hills (Psalm 50:10)

Quiz 19: **Stars in the Sky**

1. Abraham (Genesis 15:3–5)
2. Deborah, Barak (Judges 5:1, 20)
3. wise men from the east (Matthew 2:1–2)
4. True (Psalm 147:4)
5. consider (Psalm 8:3)

Quiz 20: **Honey**

1. Canaan (Numbers 13:17, 27)
2. Saul's son Jonathan (1 Samuel 14:24–30)
3. Samson (Judges 14:5–8)
4. True (Revelation 10:8–10)
5. words (Proverbs 16:24)

Quiz 21: **Fruit**
1. grapes (Numbers 13:23)
2. figs (2 Kings 20:7)
3. olives (Leviticus 24:2)
4. True (Revelation 22:2)
5. apples (Proverbs 25:11)

Quiz 22: **Cups**
1. Pharaoh's chief butler (Genesis 40:11–13)
2. Benjamin (Genesis 44:12)
3. His blood of the new testament (Mark 14:23–24)
4. True (Luke 22:42)
5. runneth (Psalm 23:5)

Quiz 23: **Chariots**
1. Joseph (Genesis 46:29)
2. Elijah (2 Kings 2:11)
3. an Ethiopian eunuch (Acts 8:27–28)
4. Trick. It was Jehu (2 Kings 9:20)
5. remember (Psalm 20:7)

Quiz 24: **Wind**
1. Elijah (1 Kings 19:11–13)
2. True (Mark 4:38–39)
3. the Holy Ghost (Acts 2:1–4)
4. angels (Revelation 7:1)
5. listeth (John 3:8)

Quiz 25: **Wells**
1. Midian (Exodus 2:15)
2. Hagar (Genesis 16:7–14)
3. Jacob (Genesis 29:3–10)
4. Trick. It was Isaac (Genesis 26:17–22)
5. Jesus (John 4:6)

Quiz 26: **Doors**

1. Ehud (Judges 3:21–25)
2. Jephthah (Judges 11:30–31)
3. Samson (Judges 16:3)
4. Trick. David did that (1 Samuel 21:12–13)
5. night (Acts 5:19)

Quiz 27: **Hair**

1. Samson (Judges 16:17)
2. Absalom (2 Samuel 14:25–26)
3. Trick. It was because of a vow (Acts 18:18–19)
4. Jesus, the Son of man (Revelation 1:13–14)
5. numbered (Matthew 10:30)

Quiz 28: **Windows**

1. one (Genesis 6:16)
2. Rahab (Joshua 2:1–15)
3. Eutychus (Acts 20:9)
4. True (Genesis 26:8)
5. face (2 Kings 9:30)

Quiz 29: **Trees**

1. almond (Numbers 17:8)
2. True (1 Kings 5:6)
3. oak (1 Kings 13:14)
4. sycomore (Luke 19:2–4)
5. palm (John 12:13)

Quiz 30: **Barley**

1. Absalom (2 Samuel 14:29–30)
2. Hosea (Hosea 3:1–2)
3. True (Judges 7:13–14)
4. five (John 6:9)
5. winnoweth (Ruth 3:2)

Quiz 31: **Pools**

1. True (2 Samuel 4:11–12)
2. Ahab (1 Kings 22:37–39)
3. Hezekiah (2 Kings 20:20)
4. an angel (John 5:2–4)
5. Sent (John 9:7)

Quiz 32: **Red**

1. Esau (Genesis 25:25)
2. dry land (Exodus 14:29)
3. True (Exodus 26:14)
4. to take peace from the earth so that people should kill one another (Revelation 6:4)
5. reason (Isaiah 1:18)

Quiz 33: **Grass**

1. the third (Genesis 1:11–13)
2. King Ahab (1 Kings 18:2–5)
3. Trick. God did that to Nebuchadnezzar (Daniel 4:33)
4. all of it (Revelation 8:7)
5. fadeth (Isaiah 40:8)

Quiz 34: **Shoes**

1. Moses (Exodus 3:4–5)
2. the Passover lamb (Exodus 12:3, 11)
3. Joshua (Joshua 9:3–6)
4. True (Luke 15:22)
5. repentance (Matthew 3:11)

Quiz 35: **You Bug Me!**

1. worms (Exodus 16:20)
2. grasshoppers (Numbers 13:33)
3. locusts (Matthew 3:4)
4. Trick. They should learn from the ant (Proverbs 6:6–8)
5. spider (Proverbs 30:28)

Quiz 36: **You Bug Me Again!**
1. flies (Exodus 8:24)
2. True (1 Samuel 24:14)
3. hornets (Exodus 23:28)
4. moth (Matthew 6:19)
5. gnat (Matthew 23:24)

Quiz 37: **Speaking of Camels...**
1. Isaac (Genesis 24:63-65)
2. Joseph (Genesis 37:25-28)
3. True (Judges 8:21)
4. the queen of Sheba (1 Kings 10:1-2)
5. eye (Matthew 19:24)

Quiz 38: **Myrrh**
1. Esther (Esther 2:12)
2. as holy anointing oil (Exodus 30:23-25)
3. gold and frankincense (Matthew 2:11)
4. Trick. It was wine mingled with myrrh (Mark 15:23)
5. Nicodemus (John 19:39)

Quiz 39: **Thrones**
1. Solomon (1 Kings 10:16-19)
2. Bathsheba, his mother (1 Kings 2:19)
3. Herod (Acts 12:21-23)
4. True (Revelation 4:2-3)
5. holy (Psalm 11:4)

Quiz 40: **Oil**
1. five (Matthew 25:2-3)
2. Trick. This miracle occurred with Elijah (1 Kings 17:12-16)
3. wine (Luke 10:33-34)
4. Jacob (Genesis 28:18)
5. Samuel (1 Samuel 10:1)

Quiz 41: **Harps**

1. Jubal (Genesis 4:21)
2. David (1 Samuel 16:23)
3. Saul (1 Samuel 10:5, 10–11)
4. True (Revelation 15:2)
5. sing (Psalm 33:2)

Quiz 42: **Sleep**

1. Sisera (Judges 4:18–21)
2. Elijah (1 Kings 19:2–6)
3. Jonah (Jonah 1:5)
4. True (Mark 4:38)
5. sustained (Psalm 3:5)

Quiz 43: **Sackcloth**

1. ashes (for example, Isaiah 58:5; Jeremiah 6:26; Luke 10:13)
2. Trick: Ahab was scared, put on sackcloth, and humbled himself before the Lord (1 Kings 21:27)
3. Haman (Esther 3:12–13, 4:1)
4. Nineveh (Jonah 3:5–8)
5. anger (Jeremiah 4:8)

Quiz 44: **Robes**

1. David (1 Chronicles 15:2, 27)
2. King Jehoshaphat of Judah (1 Kings 22:30)
3. Joseph (Genesis 37:3)
4. True (John 19:2)
5. white (Revelation 6:11)

Quiz 45: **Dancing**

1. Miriam, Moses' sister (Exodus 15:20)
2. David (2 Samuel 6:13–14)
3. King Saul (1 Samuel 18:6–8)
4. True (Exodus 32:19)
5. mourning (Psalm 30:11)

Quiz 46: **Baskets**

1. three (Genesis 40:16)
2. an angel of the Lord (Judges 6:11, 20)
3. Trick. Twelve baskets remained (Matthew 14:20)
4. the converted persecutor Saul (Acts 9:24–25)
5. pitch (Exodus 2:3)

Quiz 47: **Salt**

1. Lot's wife (Genesis 19:23–26)
2. True (Leviticus 2:13)
3. Abimelech (Judges 9:45)
4. Elisha (2 Kings 2:19–21)
5. earth (Matthew 5:13)

Quiz 48: **Clouds**

1. True (Numbers 9:15)
2. seven (1 Kings 18:44)
3. the Son of man (Mark 14:62)
4. the Lord (1 Thessalonians 4:16–17)
5. chariot (Psalm 104:3)

Quiz 49: **Writing**

1. God (Exodus 32:16)
2. the unembodied fingers of a man's hand (Daniel 5:5, 25)
3. Zacharias (Luke 1:59–63)
4. True (John 19:19)
5. Moses (Deuteronomy 31:24)

Quiz 50: **Time**

1. as one day (2 Peter 3:8)
2. for seasons (Psalm 104:19)
3. Trick. It's today! (2 Corinthians 6:2)
4. a vapour (James 4:14)
5. purpose (Ecclesiastes 3:1)

Quiz 51: **Seven**

1. God (Genesis 2:3)
2. Mary Magdalene (Luke 8:2)
3. a rain cloud (1 Kings 18:43–44)
4. Trick. He agreed to work to marry Rachel (Genesis 29:18)
5. thunders (Revelation 10:3)

Quiz 52: **Lions**

1. Judah (Genesis 49:9)
2. David (1 Samuel 17:34–36)
3. True (1 Kings 13:24–26)
4. Samson (Judges 14:5)
5. seeking (1 Peter 5:8)

Quiz 53: **Sheep**

1. Abel (Genesis 4:2)
2. Trick. It was Jacob (Genesis 30:37–39)
3. caught in a thicket (Genesis 22:13)
4. King David (2 Samuel 12:1–7)
5. astray (Isaiah 53:6)

Quiz 54: **Thieves**

1. the Philistines (1 Samuel 5:1–2)
2. Dan (Judges 18:1, 18–20)
3. Jacob (Genesis 27:35–36)
4. True (Genesis 31:19)
5. destroy (John 10:10)

Quiz 55: **Brass**

1. Judah's King Zedekiah (2 Kings 25:7)
2. True (Deuteronomy 28:23)
3. Goliath (1 Samuel 17:4–5)
4. a serpent (Numbers 21:8–9)
5. shoes (Deuteronomy 33:25)

Quiz 56: **Teeth**
1. quail (Numbers 11:32–33)
2. Trick. Job said that (Job 19:20)
3. ribs (Daniel 7:5)
4. gravel stones (Lamentations 3:16)
5. wailing (Matthew 13:42)

Quiz 57: **Beards**
1. shaved them half off (2 Samuel 10:3–4)
2. Aaron's (Psalm 133:2)
3. Mephibosheth (2 Samuel 19:24)
4. True (Isaiah 50:6)
5. plucked (Ezra 9:3)

Quiz 58: **Posts**
1. lamb's blood (Exodus 12:21–23)
2. God's words (Deuteronomy 6:6–9)
3. Trick. He carried them to a hilltop (Judges 16:3)
4. Isaiah (Isaiah 6:1–4)
5. gates (Proverbs 8:34)

Quiz 59: **Eyes**
1. True (1 Samuel 16:7)
2. horses and chariots of fire (2 Kings 6:17)
3. men as trees, walking (Mark 8:23–24)
4. scales (Acts 9:18)
5. Open (Psalm 119:18)

Quiz 60: **Nostrils**
1. when God breathed the breath of life into his nostrils (Genesis 2:7)
2. all on dry land in whose nostrils was the breath of life (Genesis 7:22)
3. Job (Job 27:3)
4. True (Numbers 11:20)
5. blast (Job 4:9)

Quiz 61: **Crowns**
1. incorruptible (1 Corinthians 9:25)
2. True (1 Thessalonians 2:19–20)
3. crown of righteousness (2 Timothy 4:8)
4. crown of glory (1 Peter 5:2–4)
5. life (James 1:12)

Quiz 62: **Barren Women**
1. Trick. Abraham took matters into his own hands, but Isaac prayed (Genesis 16:1–4, 25:21)
2. Rachel (Genesis 29:31)
3. Manoah's wife (Judges 13:2, 24)
4. Hannah (1 Samuel 1:5, 20)
5. Elisabeth (Luke 1:7)

Quiz 63: **Birds of a Feather**
1. the fifth (Genesis 1:20–23)
2. a raven (Genesis 8:7)
3. True (Deuteronomy 14:12, 19)
4. sparrows (Matthew 10:31)
5. peacocks (1 Kings 10:22)

Quiz 64: **Grandpas**
1. Boaz (Ruth 4:21–22)
2. True (Genesis 5:25–29)
3. Abraham (Genesis 25:19–26)
4. Reuben, Simeon, Levi, Judah, Issachar, Zebulun, Dan, Joseph, Benjamin, Naphtali, Gad, and Asher (1 Chronicles 2:1–2)
5. Lot (Genesis 11:31)

Quiz 65: **Quakes and Twisters and Hail—Oh My!**
1. Trick. It was Korah's family; Keturah was Abraham's second wife (Numbers 16:31–33)
2. wind (Job 1:19)
3. hail (Exodus 9:18)
4. hailstones (Joshua 10:11)
5. an earthquake (Matthew 27:50–51)

Quiz 66: **Inns**
1. a Samaritan in a parable of Jesus (Luke 10:33–34)
2. Trick: They were Jacob's sons (Genesis 42:27–29)
3. Moses (Exodus 4:21–25)
4. Mary (Luke 2:5–7)
5. Rahab (Joshua 2:1)

Quiz 67: **Raised From the Dead**
1. Peter (Acts 9:36–41)
2. Elijah (1 Kings 17:17–24)
3. Paul (Acts 20:9–12)
4. True (2 Kings 13:20–21)
5. face (John 11:43–44)

Quiz 68: **Kings**
1. Manasseh (2 Kings 21:1)
2. True (1 Kings 16:15)
3. Joash (2 Chronicles 24:1)
4. David (2 Samuel 5:5)
5. rejected (1 Samuel 8:7)

Quiz 69: **False Gods**
1. Dagon of the Philistines (1 Samuel 5:1–4)
2. True (Psalm 135:15–18)
3. graven (Exodus 20:4)
4. a calf (Exodus 32:8)
5. Asa of Judah (1 Kings 15:13)

Quiz 70: **Flowers**
1. rose (Song of Solomon 2:1)
2. lilies (Matthew 6:28–29)
3. True (1 Kings 6:18)
4. Aaron's (Numbers 17:8)
5. the word of our God (Isaiah 40:8)

Quiz 71: **Smoke, Clouds, and Fire**
1. Trick: He appeared to Abram that way (Genesis 15:17–18)
2. Moses (Exodus 3:2–3)
3. the Israelites in the wilderness (Exodus 13:19–21)
4. cloven tongues of fire (Acts 2:1–4)
5. brightness (Ezekiel 10:4)

Quiz 72: **God's Covenants**
1. food from plants and trees (Genesis 1:29–30)
2. flood the entire earth (Genesis 9:9–13)
3. Trick. Abraham's descendants weren't guaranteed eternal security (Genesis 12:1–3; John 8:33–40)
4. an eternal kingdom (2 Samuel 7:15–16)
5. blood (Matthew 26:28)

Quiz 73: **Creation**
1. six (Genesis 1:31)
2. True (Genesis 1:31)
3. "in his own image" (Genesis 1:27)
4. the sixth (Genesis 1:26–31)
5. subdue (Genesis 1:28)

Quiz 74: **What a Woman!**
1. alone (Genesis 2:18)
2. "help meet" (Genesis 2:18)
3. Trick. God took a rib from Adam to create her (Genesis 2:22)
4. because she was the mother of all living (Genesis 3:20)
5. naked (Genesis 2:25)

Quiz 75: **The First Sin**
1. the serpent (Genesis 3:1)
2. a tree (Genesis 2:17)
3. fig (Genesis 3:7)
4. True (Genesis 3:17–18)
5. flaming (Genesis 3:24)

Quiz 76: **The First Murder**

1. Trick. He was a tiller of the ground (Genesis 4:2)
2. keeper of sheep (Genesis 4:2)
3. Abel's firstlings of his flock (Genesis 4:4–5)
4. in a field (Genesis 4:8)
5. sin (Genesis 4:7)

Quiz 77: **Noah**

1. three (Genesis 6:16)
2. six hundred years old (Genesis 7:11)
3. earth (Genesis 7:12)
4. True (Genesis 7:20)
5. the mountains of Ararat (Genesis 8:4)

Quiz 78: **The Tower of Babel**

1. True (Genesis 11:1)
2. that they'd be scattered across the earth (Genesis 11:4)
3. city (Genesis 11:4)
4. by confounding their language (Genesis 11:6–8)
5. Shinar (Genesis 11:2)

Quiz 79: **Abraham**

1. one hundred years old (Genesis 21:5)
2. his servant Eliezer (Genesis 15:2–3)
3. hard (Genesis 18:14)
4. Trick. Ishmael was his firstborn, by Sarah's servant (Genesis 16:15–16)
5. Melchizedek (Genesis 14:18–20)

Quiz 80: **Lot and Abraham Separate**

1. Trick. It was because of strife between their herdsmen (Genesis 13:7)
2. because both of them had a lot of cattle (Genesis 13:2, 5–6)
3. the plain of Jordan, toward Sodom (Genesis 13:11–12)
4. the land of Canaan (Genesis 13:12)
5. depart (Genesis 13:9)

Quiz 81: **Abraham's Sons**

1. Hagar (Genesis 16:15)
2. as many as the stars in the sky (Genesis 15:5)
3. Trick. He was a hundred years old (Genesis 21:5)
4. sent them away (Genesis 21:12-14)
5. blessed (Genesis 12:3)

Quiz 82: **Sodom and Gomorrah**

1. two angels (Genesis 19:1-3)
2. struck them with blindness (Genesis 19:11)
3. behind them (Genesis 19:17)
4. True (Genesis 19:26)
5. furnace (Genesis 19:28)

Quiz 83: **Talk about a Sacrifice!**

1. Trick. He obeyed immediately (Genesis 22:2-3)
2. Moriah (Genesis 22:2)
3. bind him (Genesis 22:9)
4. a ram (Genesis 22:13)
5. blessing (Genesis 22:16-17)

Quiz 84: **Rebekah**

1. Isaac (Genesis 24:67)
2. the Canaanites (Genesis 24:3)
3. True (Genesis 24:12-14)
4. Laban (Genesis 24:29)
5. mother (Genesis 24:60)

Quiz 85: **Selling the Birthright**

1. Trick. The opposite was true (Genesis 25:28)
2. hunting (Genesis 25:27)
3. Esau (Genesis 25:34)
4. bread and pottage of lentils (Genesis 25:34)
5. die (Genesis 25:32)

Quiz 86: **Stolen Blessing**

1. blindness (Genesis 27:1)
2. Rebekah (Genesis 27:5)
3. hairy hands, clothes that had Esau's scent (Genesis 27:23, 27)
4. True (Genesis 27:22)
5. one (Genesis 27:38)

Quiz 87: **Jacob's Ladder**

1. while he was dreaming (Genesis 28:12)
2. the angels of God (Genesis 28:12)
3. Trick. The lower end rested on the earth (Genesis 28:12)
4. Bethel (Genesis 28:19)
5. afraid (Genesis 28:17)

Quiz 88: **The Case of the Two Wives**

1. Rachel (Genesis 29:18)
2. his uncle, Laban, the girls' father (Genesis 29:25–26)
3. gave Jacob their personal slaves in hopes of having children through them (Genesis 30:3, 9)
4. True (Genesis 35:21–26)
5. multiply (Genesis 35:11)

Quiz 89: **Dinah**

1. Trick. She was Jacob's daughter (Genesis 34:1)
2. Shechem the Hivite (Genesis 34:2)
3. marry Shechem (Genesis 34:4, 8)
4. Simeon and Levi (Genesis 34:25)
5. stink (Genesis 34:30)

Quiz 90: **Joseph's Dreams**

1. two (Genesis 37:5, 9)
2. bowing before Joseph (Genesis 37:7–10)
3. Trick. They hated him even more (Genesis 37:8)
4. rebuked Joseph (Genesis 37:10)
5. Hear (Genesis 37:6)

Quiz 91: **Joseph Sold into Slavery**

1. Rueben (Genesis 37:21–22)
2. Judah (Genesis 37:26–27)
3. Trick. They were Ishmaelite/Midianite traders who were going to Egypt (Genesis 37:27–28)
4. twenty (Genesis 37:28)
5. goats (Genesis 37:31)

Quiz 92: **Joseph's Owner, Potiphar**

1. prosperous (Genesis 39:2)
2. because he was "well favoured," or handsome (Genesis 39:6–7)
3. True (Genesis 39:12)
4. prison (Genesis 39:20)
5. the Lord (Genesis 39:21)

Quiz 93: **Prisoner Dreams**

1. butler, baker (Genesis 40:1)
2. three days (Genesis 40:12, 18)
3. both (Genesis 40:21–22)
4. Trick. He forgot about Joseph (Genesis 40:23)
5. interpretations (Genesis 40:8)

Quiz 94: **Job the Blessed**

1. Uz (Job 1:1)
2. ten—seven sons and three daughters (Job 1:2)
3. True (Job 1:4)
4. offer burnt offerings (Job 1:5)
5. feared (Job 1:1)

Quiz 95: **Job's First Test**

1. Satan and the sons of God (Job 1:6)
2. True (Job 1:12)
3. they were taken by the Chaldeans (Job 1:17)
4. a great wind that collapsed the house on them (Job 1:19)
5. blessed (Job 1:21)

Quiz 96: **Job's Second Test**

1. the earth (Job 2:2)
2. Job's health (Job 2:5)
3. Trick. She told him to curse God, and die (Job 2:9)
4. three (Job 2:11)
5. ashes (Job 2:8)

Quiz 97: **Miserable Comforters**

1. True (Job 32:3, 42:7)
2. a whirlwind (Job 38:1)
3. Pleiades, Orion (Job 38:31)
4. offer burnt offerings and have Job pray for them (Job 42:8)
5. thought (Job 42:2)

Quiz 98: **The End of Job's Story**

1. True (Job 42:10)
2. a piece of money, a gold earring (Job 42:11)
3. more than anyone else (Job 42:15)
4. 140 (Job 42:16)
5. blessed (Job 42:12)

Quiz 99: **Baby Moses**

1. Levi (Exodus 2:1)
2. three months (Exodus 2:2–3)
3. True (Exodus 2:10)
4. his real mother (Exodus 2:7–8)
5. sister (Exodus 2:4)

Quiz 100: **Moses the Young Man**

1. True (Exodus 2:11–12)
2. seven (Exodus 2:16)
3. Zipporah (Exodus 2:21)
4. Gershom (Exodus 2:22)
5. because of their bondage in Egypt (Exodus 2:23)

Quiz 101: **Moses the Shepherd**

1. Horeb (Exodus 3:1)
2. a bush (Exodus 3:2)
3. hid his face (Exodus 3:6)
4. True (Exodus 3:11–4:13)
5. mouth (Exodus 4:12)

Quiz 102: **Moses, God's Spokesman**

1. Trick: He took them with him (Exodus 4:20)
2. the Lord (Exodus 4:24)
3. Aaron, his brother (Exodus 4:27)
4. yes (Exodus 4:31)
5. harden (Exodus 4:21)

Quiz 103: **The Ten Plagues**

1. blood (Exodus 7:17)
2. Pharaoh's magicians (Exodus 9:11)
3. Pharaoh and God (Exodus 8:15, 10:1)
4. three (Exodus 10:22)
5. Trick. God included them in His judgment (Exodus 11:5)

Quiz 104: **Tabernacle Items**

1. brass altar, brass laver (Exodus 27:1–2, 30:18)
2. the shewbread table (Exodus 25:23–30)
3. a golden candlestick (Exodus 25:31–37)
4. Trick. The ark of the covenant was behind the veil (Exodus 26:33–34)
5. incense (Exodus 30:1)

Quiz 105: **Tabernacle and Temple Offerings**

1. a burnt sacrifice (Leviticus 1:3, 10)
2. True (Leviticus 2:1)
3. the altar (Leviticus 6:9)
4. the ashes (Leviticus 4:2–12)
5. atonement (Leviticus 5:6)

Quiz 106: **The Twelve Spies**

1. Canaan (Numbers 13:2)
2. two (Numbers 13:23)
3. True (Numbers 13:32–33)
4. two (Numbers 14:6–8)
5. bring (Numbers 14:8)

Quiz 107: **Fiery Serpents Incident**

1. for speaking against God (Numbers 21:5–6)
2. died (Numbers 21:6)
3. pray for them (Numbers 21:7)
4. God (Numbers 21:8)
5. True (Numbers 21:8–9)

Quiz 108: **Balaam**

1. Trick. Balak was the king of the Moabites (Numbers 22:4–6)
2. God (Numbers 22:9–12)
3. his donkey (Numbers 22:28)
4. the angel of the Lord (Numbers 22:31–33)
5. sinned (Numbers 22:34)

Quiz 109: **Rahab**

1. two (Joshua 2:4)
2. on the roof, among stalks of flax (Joshua 2:6)
3. Trick. She had to give the Israelites a sign (Joshua 2:12–18)
4. a scarlet thread (Joshua 2:18)
5. terror (Joshua 2:9)

Quiz 110: **Crossing the Jordan**

1. when the priests' feet touched the edge of the water (Joshua 3:13, 15)
2. True (Joshua 3:15)
3. on dry ground in the middle of the river (Joshua 3:17)
4. twelve (Joshua 4:2–7)
5. Joshua (Joshua 4:14)

Quiz 111: **The Walls of Jericho**

1. once (Joshua 6:3)
2. Trick. The Bible doesn't say what they shouted (Joshua 6:10)
3. they were supposed to march in total silence (Joshua 6:10)
4. only her father's family (Joshua 6:23–25)
5. flat (Joshua 6:20)

Quiz 112: **Achan**

1. stealing plunder from Jericho, which God had forbidden (Joshua 7:1)
2. he was stoned then burned with fire (Joshua 7:25)
3. True (Joshua 7:11–12)
4. Ai (Joshua 7:5)
5. destroy (Joshua 7:12)

Quiz 113: **Deception!**

1. The inhabitants of Gibeon (Joshua 9:3–15)
2. True (Joshua 9:4–5)
3. three days (Joshua 9:16)
4. because they'd sworn an oath before the Lord (Joshua 9:18–19)
5. beguiled (Joshua 9:22)

Quiz 114: **An Unnatural Phenomenon**

1. Trick. They fought against Gibeon, which had a treaty with Israel (Joshua 10:4–5)
2. great stones (Joshua 10:11)
3. for the sun and moon to stand still (Joshua 10:12–13)
4. after the Israelites won the battle (Joshua 10:13)
5. voice (Joshua 10:14)

Quiz 115: **Ehud**

1. Eglon (Judges 3:14–15)
2. he was lefthanded (Judges 3:15, 21)
3. True (Judges 3:24–25)
4. about ten thousand (Judges 3:29)
5. Moabites (Judges 3:28)

Quiz 116: **Deborah and Barak**

1. twenty (Judges 4:3)
2. a palm (Judges 4:5)
3. day (Judges 4:14)
4. Jael, wife of Heber the Kenite (Judges 4:17–19)
5. True (Judges 4:21)

Quiz 117: **Gideon's Wet Blanket**

1. to hide it from the Midianites (Judges 6:11)
2. deliver Israel from the Midianites (Judges 6:14)
3. Trick. His family was the weakest, and he was the youngest (Judges 6:15)
4. two (Judges 6:36–40)
5. valour (Judges 6:12)

Quiz 118: **God Handpicks Gideon's Army**

1. Jerubbaal (Judges 7:1)
2. two times (Judges 7:3–5)
3. True (Judges 7:5)
4. three hundred (Judges 7:6–7)
5. many (Judges 7:2)

Quiz 119: **The Battle That Never Actually Occurred**

1. three (Judges 7:16)
2. a trumpet, an empty pitcher, and a lamp (inside the pitcher) (Judges 7:16)
3. Trick. The Israelites blew the trumpets and broke the pitchers, revealing the light of the lamps (Judges 7:20)
4. He "set every man's sword against his fellow" (Judges 7:22)
5. Midian (Judges 7:15)

Quiz 120: **Samson and Delilah**

1. True (Judges 16:5)
2. eleven hundred (Judges 16:5)
3. three times (Judges 16:6-15)
4. a Nazarite (Judges 16:17)
5. departed (Judges 16:20)

Quiz 121: **Samson the Prisoner**

1. put out his eyes (Judge 16:21)
2. Trick. The god was Dagon (Judges 16:23)
3. pillars (Judges 16:29-30)
4. twenty (Judges 16:31)
5. strengthen (Judges 16:28)

Quiz 122: **Ruth**

1. Naomi (Ruth 1:2-6)
2. Moabite (Ruth 1:4)
3. True (Ruth 2:5-9, 4:10)
4. God (Ruth 1:16)
5. at his feet (Ruth 3:7-9)

Quiz 123: **Hannah**

1. because she was barren (1 Samuel 1:6-8)
2. that she was drunk (1 Samuel 1:13-14)
3. Trick. She had a son first (1 Samuel 1:19-20)
4. dedicated him to the Lord by having him live at the tabernacle (1 Samuel 1:22-28)
5. rock (1 Samuel 2:2)

Quiz 124: **Samuel's Call**

1. nighttime (1 Samuel 3:2-4)
2. Eli (1 Samuel 3:4-8)
3. Trick. It took four times (1 Samuel 3:4-10)
4. Speak (1 Samuel 3:10)
5. Eli's family (1 Samuel 3:12-14)

Quiz 125: **Captured Ark**
1. the Philistines (1 Samuel 4:10–11)
2. Trick. This happened to the false idol Dagon (1 Samuel 5:4)
3. because wherever the ark went, the Lord afflicted everyone there (1 Samuel 5:7–9)
4. return it to the Israelites (1 Samuel 5:11)
5. emerods (1 Samuel 5:12)

Quiz 126: **Returned Ark**
1. True (1 Samuel 6:7)
2. the plagues God had sent on Pharaoh for hardening his heart (1 Samuel 6:6)
3. Bethshemesh (1 Samuel 6:12–13)
4. because they looked into the ark of the Lord (1 Samuel 6:19)
5. holy (1 Samuel 6:20)

Quiz 127: **Israel's First King**
1. Saul (1 Samuel 9:27–10:1)
2. his donkeys (1 Samuel 9:3)
3. Trick. He was very tall (1 Samuel 9:2)
4. hiding "among the stuff," or supplies (1 Samuel 10:22)
5. rejected (1 Samuel 10:19)

Quiz 128: **Jabesh-Gilead**
1. cut out everyone's right eye (1 Samuel 11:2)
2. seven days (1 Samuel 11:3)
3. Saul (1 Samuel 11:6)
4. morning (1 Samuel 11:11)
5. Trick. There were a few survivors, but they were scattered entirely apart (1 Samuel 11:11)

Quiz 129: **The Giant**
1. the Philistines (1 Samuel 17:4)
2. forty (1 Samuel 17:16)
3. one (1 Samuel 17:48–49)
4. hosts (1 Samuel 17:45)
5. Trick. He used Goliath's sword (1 Samuel 17:51)

Quiz 130: **David's Wives**

1. True (1 Samuel 18:20, 27)
2. Abigail (1 Samuel 25:37–42)
3. Bathsheba (2 Samuel 11:3–5, 26–27)
4. Bathsheba (2 Samuel 12:24; 1 Kings 1:28–30)
5. die (2 Samuel 12:13)

Quiz 131: **David Spares Saul's Life**

1. three thousand (1 Samuel 24:2)
2. True (1 Samuel 24:3)
3. cut off the skirt of Saul's robe (1 Samuel 24:4)
4. "more righteous than I" (1 Samuel 24:17)
5. hand (1 Samuel 24:12)

Quiz 132: **Woman with a Familiar Spirit**

1. Endor (1 Samuel 28:7)
2. True (1 Samuel 28:8)
3. Samuel (1 Samuel 28:11)
4. dead, with him (1 Samuel 28:19)
5. wizards (1 Samuel 28:9)

Quiz 133: **Civil War**

1. Saul (2 Samuel 3:1)
2. Hebron (2 Samuel 3:2)
3. Abner (2 Samuel 3:8–11)
4. True (2 Samuel 3:13)
5. foreskins (2 Samuel 3:14)

Quiz 134: **Abner's Assassination**

1. Trick. David accepted Abner, while his commander Joab distrusted him as a spy (2 Samuel 3:23–25)
2. Hebron (2 Samuel 3:27)
3. the fifth (2 Samuel 3:27)
4. Asahel, Joab's brother, who had been killed in battle by Abner (2 Samuel 3:27)
5. guiltless (2 Samuel 3:28)

Quiz 135: **Assassination of a King**
1. Ishbosheth (2 Samuel 2:8-9)
2. True (2 Samuel 4:5-7)
3. King David of Judah (2 Samuel 4:8)
4. they were killed, and hung over a pool in Hebron (2 Samuel 4:12)
5. blood (2 Samuel 4:11)

Quiz 136: **David Conquers Jerusalem**
1. the Jebusites (2 Samuel 5:6)
2. Trick. The Jebusites mentioned the blind and the *lame* (2 Samuel 5:6)
3. they climbed up the gutter (2 Samuel 5:8)
4. thirty-three (2 Samuel 5:5)
5. great (2 Samuel 5:10)

Quiz 137: **Absalom Murders Amnon**
1. half brothers (2 Samuel 3:2-3)
2. for violating Absalom's full sister Tamar (2 Samuel 13:11)
3. True (2 Samuel 13:28)
4. they fled (2 Samuel 13:29)
5. earth (2 Samuel 13:31)

Quiz 138: **Absalom's Rebellion**
1. Trick. He would pull them up as they bowed to him, and kiss them (2 Samuel 15:5-6)
2. Hebron (2 Samuel 15:7)
3. trumpet (2 Samuel 15:10)
4. fled Jerusalem (2 Samuel 15:14)
5. Ahithophel (2 Samuel 15:12)

Quiz 139: **David Leaves Jerusalem**
1. True (2 Samuel 15:24-26)
2. Ziba, servant of Mephibosheth (2 Samuel 16:1-2)
3. Shimei (2 Samuel 16:5-13)
4. affliction (2 Samuel 16:12)
5. a tent (2 Samuel 16:22)

Quiz 140: **King Absalom**

1. twelve thousand (2 Samuel 17:1)
2. Hushai (2 Samuel 17:7-13)
3. True (2 Samuel 17:16-21)
4. in a well (2 Samuel 17:18-19)
5. evil (2 Samuel 17:14)

Quiz 141: **Absalom's Defeat**

1. the wood of Ephraim (2 Samuel 18:6)
2. Trick. He was riding a mule (2 Samuel 18:9)
3. because David ordered that no one was to harm Absalom (2 Samuel 18:12)
4. thrust three darts through his heart (2 Samuel 18:14)
5. dead (2 Samuel 18:20)

Quiz 142: **The Lord and Solomon**

1. True (1 Kings 3:3)
2. Gibeon (1 Kings 3:5)
3. long life, riches, the death of his enemies (1 Kings 3:11)
4. in a dream (1 Kings 3:5, 15)
5. feast (1 Kings 3:15)

Quiz 143: **Two Moms, One Baby**

1. Trick. They were harlots (1 Kings 3:16-22)
2. a sword (1 Kings 3:24)
3. cut it in two and give one half to each woman (1 Kings 3:25)
4. "O my lord, give her the living child, and in no wise slay it" (1 Kings 3:26)
5. wisdom (1 Kings 3:28)

Quiz 144: **The Queen of Sheba**

1. with hard questions (1 Kings 10:1)
2. camels (1 Kings 10:2)
3. True (1 Kings 10:6-7)
4. all she desired, along with some of his royal bounty (1 Kings 10:13)
5. delighted (1 Kings 10:9)

Quiz 145: **The Man with Many Wives**

1. seven hundred (1 Kings 11:3)
2. three hundred (1 Kings 11:3)
3. True (1 Kings 11:4–5)
4. divide Israel into two kingdoms (1 Kings 11:11–13)
5. heart (1 Kings 11:2)

Quiz 146: **A Kingdom Divided**

1. Jeroboam and all the congregation of Israel (1 Kings 12:3–4)
2. three (1 Kings 12:5)
3. True (1 Kings 12:8, 14)
4. the cities of Judah (1 Kings 12:17)
5. rebelled (1 Kings 12:19)

Quiz 147: **Attempted Reunification**

1. stoned by the Israelites (1 Kings 12:18)
2. True (1 Kings 12:21)
3. Benjamin (1 Kings 12:21)
4. the Lord (1 Kings 12:24)
5. David (1 Kings 12:20)

Quiz 148: **Jeroboam's Idolatry**

1. two calves of gold (1 Kings 12:26–28)
2. True (1 Kings 12:26–27)
3. brought the people out of Egypt (1 Kings 12:28)
4. Bethel, Dan (1 Kings 12:29)
5. gods (1 Kings 12:28)

Quiz 149: **The Man of God and Jeroboam**

1. True (1 Kings 13:1–3)
2. his hand (1 Kings 13:4)
3. ask God to restore him (1 Kings 13:6)
4. the Lord (1 Kings 13:9)
5. ashes (1 Kings 13:5)

Quiz 150: **Elijah and the Widow**

1. sticks (1 Kings 17:10)
2. a cake, or bread (1 Kings 17:12)
3. True (1 Kings 17:13)
4. her barrel of flour and jug of oil never ran out (1 Kings 17:14)
5. eat (1 Kings 17:15)

Quiz 151: **Elijah at Mount Carmel**

1. four hundred and fifty (1 Kings 18:22)
2. True (1 Kings 18:23–24)
3. all day, from morning until the time for the evening sacrifice (1 Kings 18:26–29)
4. water (1 Kings 18:33–35)
5. opinions (1 Kings 18:21)

Quiz 152: **Elijah and God at Horeb**

1. Trick. She planned to kill him (1 Kings 19:1–2)
2. a juniper tree (1 Kings 19:4)
3. life (1 Kings 19:4)
4. a strong wind, an earthquake, a fire (1 Kings 19:11–12)
5. True (1 Kings 19:15–18)

Quiz 153: **Naboth's Vineyard**

1. King Ahab (1 Kings 21:2)
2. Queen Jezebel (1 Kings 21:7–8)
3. True (1 Kings 21:12–13)
4. he was stoned to death (1 Kings 21:13)
5. dogs (1 Kings 21:19)

Quiz 154: **Death of a Nasty Queen**

1. Jehu (2 Kings 9:30)
2. True (2 Kings 9:33)
3. rode over her dead body, went inside, and ate and drank (2 Kings 9:33–34)
4. the skull, the feet, the palms of her hands (2 Kings 9:35)
5. dung (2 Kings 9:37)

Quiz 155: **Miracle of Multiplication**

1. a widow of one of the prophets (2 Kings 4:1)
2. Trick. They threatened to take her two sons (2 Kings 4:1)
3. vessels, or empty jars (2 Kings 4:3)
4. oil (2 Kings 4:4–6)
5. live (2 Kings 4:7)

Quiz 156: **Poisoned Food**

1. herbs (2 Kings 4:39)
2. wild gourds (2 Kings 4:39)
3. True (2 Kings 4:40)
4. meal, or flour (2 Kings 4:41)
5. pot (2 Kings 4:41)

Quiz 157: **Multiplied Bread Loaves**

1. barley (2 Kings 4:42)
2. twenty (2 Kings 4:42)
3. one hundred (2 Kings 4:43)
4. Trick. He just distributed the bread (2 Kings 4:42)
5. eat (2 Kings 4:44)

Quiz 158: **Naaman and the King of Israel**

1. leprosy (2 Kings 5:1)
2. a young captive Israelite girl (2 Kings 5:2-3)
3. True (2 Kings 5:5-6)
4. he thought Syria was trying to start a fight (2 Kings 5:7)
5. God (2 Kings 5:7)

Quiz 159: **Naaman and Elisha**

1. the Jordan (2 Kings 5:10)
2. seven (2 Kings 5:10)
3. True. At least at first (2 Kings 5:11-12)
4. "like unto the flesh of a little child" (2 Kings 5:14)
5. Israel (2 Kings 5:15)

Quiz 160: **Naaman and Gehazi**

1. his servant (2 Kings 5:20)
2. True (2 Kings 5:20-22)
3. in the house (2 Kings 5:24)
4. leprosy for him and his descendants forever (2 Kings 5:27)
5. heart (2 Kings 5:26)

Quiz 161: **A Floating Axe Head**

1. the Jordan river (2 Kings 6:4–5)
2. it was borrowed (2 Kings 6:5)
3. Trick. Elisha didn't tell him to do anything (2 Kings 6:6)
4. cutting wood (2 Kings 6:4)
5. iron (2 Kings 6:6)

Quiz 162: **Fiery Army**

1. True (2 Kings 6:8–12)
2. Dothan (2 Kings 6:13)
3. a huge army surrounded the city (2 Kings 6:15)
4. horses and chariots of fire (2 Kings 6:17)
5. more (2 Kings 6:16)

Quiz 163: **Blind Army**

1. Elisha (2 Kings 6:18)
2. True (2 Kings 6:20–21)
3. bread and water (2 Kings 6:22)
4. they stopped coming into the land of Israel (2 Kings 6:23)
5. captive (2 Kings 6:22)

Quiz 164: **Horrific Famine in Samaria**

1. five (2 Kings 6:25)
2. True (2 Kings 6:26–29)
3. sackcloth (2 Kings 6:30)
4. Elisha (2 Kings 6:31)
5. Lord (2 Kings 6:27)

Quiz 165: **The Famine Breaks**

1. four lepers (2 Kings 7:3–8)
2. in the deserted camp of Syrian soldiers (2 Kings 7:5–8)
3. silver, gold, and raiment (clothing) (2 Kings 7:8)
4. God sent the sound of horses and chariots, causing them to run away (2 Kings 7:6)
5. peace (2 Kings 7:9)

Quiz 166: **King Ahaziah**

1. he fell through a lattice (2 Kings 1:2)
2. Baalzebub, the god of Ekron (2 Kings 1:2)
3. Elijah (2 Kings 1:6–8)
4. Trick. The king never repented, so God's judgment was carried out (2 Kings 1:17)
5. bed (2 Kings 1:16)

Quiz 167: **Athaliah**

1. True (2 Chronicles 22:10)
2. Joash (2 Chronicles 22:11)
3. in the house of God (2 Chronicles 22:12)
4. six (2 Chronicles 22:12)
5. nurse (2 Chronicles 22:11)

Quiz 168: **Young Joash**

1. Trick. Everyone recognized the young boy as the true ruler (2 Chronicles 23:1–3)
2. the Levites (2 Chronicles 23:7)
3. King David's (2 Chronicles 23:9)
4. a crown, the testimony (or law) (2 Chronicles 23:11)
5. save (2 Chronicles 23:11)

Quiz 169: **Ousting the Queen**

1. treason (2 Chronicles 23:13)
2. the house of the Lord (2 Chronicles 23:14)
3. Trick. The people destroyed everything connected to Baal (2 Chronicles 23:17)
4. Mattan, the priest of Baal (2 Chronicles 23:17)
5. rejoiced (2 Chronicles 23:21)

Quiz 170: **Zechariah the Priest**

1. Trick. He ordered him stoned (2 Chronicles 24:20–21)
2. Zechariah's father, Jehoiada (2 Chronicles 24:15–18)
3. Joash the king (2 Chronicles 24:22)
4. murdered by his own servants (2 Chronicles 24:25)
5. forsaken (2 Chronicles 24:20)

Quiz 171: **Psalm 23**

1. the Lord (verse 1)
2. Trick. It's in the presence of enemies (verse 5)
3. the Lord's rod and staff (verse 4)
4. pastures (verse 2)
5. dwell (verse 6)

Quiz 172: **Psalm 51**

1. God (verse 4)
2. True (verse 5)
3. hyssop (verse 7)
4. a broken spirit, a contrite heart (verse 17)
5. heart (verse 10)

Quiz 173: **Psalm 139**
1. searched him, known him (verse 1)
2. True (verses 13–15)
3. God's thoughts toward him (verses 17–18)
4. praise (verse 14)
5. night (verse 12)

Quiz 174: **Proverbs 31**
1. strength, honor (verse 25)
2. her children (verse 28)
3. beauty (verse 30)
4. the poor and needy (verse 20)
5. Trick. She rises in the night hours to serve others (verse 15)

Quiz 175: **Isaiah 6**
1. Uzziah (verse 1)
2. six (verse 2)
3. Trick. The coal touched his lips so that his sin would be removed (verses 6–7)
4. "Here am I; send me" (verse 8)
5. earth (verse 3)

Quiz 176: **The Suffering Servant (Isaiah 53)**
1. sheep (verse 6)
2. True (verse 9)
3. to bear the sin of many and make intercession for the transgressors (verse 12)
4. stripes (verse 5)
5. the Lord (verse 10)

Quiz 177: **Dry Bones**

1. an open valley (Ezekiel 37:1–2)
2. Trick. Ezekiel saw this (Ezekiel 37:7–10)
3. four (Ezekiel 37:9)
4. an exceedingly great army (Ezekiel 37:10)
5. spirit (Ezekiel 37:14)

Quiz 178: **False Worship in Jerusalem**

1. his house (Ezekiel 8:1–3)
2. True (Ezekiel 8:9–10)
3. see them (Ezekiel 8:11–12)
4. weeping for the false god Tammuz (Ezekiel 8:14)
5. abominations (Ezekiel 8:13)

Quiz 179: **The Runaway Prophet**

1. Nineveh (Jonah 1:2)
2. Tarshish (Jonah 1:3)
3. Trick. They tried everything in their power to keep him alive (Jonah 1:12–15)
4. stopped raging (Jonah 1:15)
5. feared (Jonah 1:16)

Quiz 180: **The Fishy Prophet**

1. three (Jonah 1:17)
2. prayed (Jonah 2:1)
3. vomited him out (Jonah 2:10)
4. Trick. He was spit onto the dry land (Jonah 2:10)
5. remembered (Jonah 2:7)

Quiz 181: **The Obedient Prophet**

1. forty (Jonah 3:4)
2. Trick. They believed right away (Jonah 3:5)
3. removed his robes and put on sackcloth (Jonah 3:6)
4. no one—neither man nor beast (Jonah 3:7)
5. anger (Jonah 3:9)

Quiz 182: **The Angry Prophet**

1. True (Jonah 4:1–2)
2. to see what would become of it (Jonah 4:5)
3. a gourd plant (Jonah 4:6)
4. a worm (Jonah 4:7)
5. spare (Jonah 4:11)

Quiz 183: **Young Daniel**

1. Belteshazzar (Daniel 1:7)
2. Judah (Daniel 1:6)
3. True (Daniel 1:4–5)
4. ten (Daniel 1:12)
5. knowledge (Daniel 1:17)

Quiz 184: **Nebuchadnezzar's First Recorded Dream**

1. the second (Daniel 2:1)
2. True (Daniel 2:3–13)
3. pray that God would reveal the dream and its interpretation (Daniel 2:17–23)
4. iron, clay (Daniel 2:33)
5. secrets (Daniel 2:28)

Quiz 185: **Blazing Fire**

1. gold (Daniel 3:1)
2. Shadrach, Meshach, Abednego (Daniel 3:12)
3. True (Daniel 3:13-15)
4. four (Daniel 3:25)
5. furnace (Daniel 3:17)

Quiz 186: **Den of Lions**

1. praying to God (Daniel 6:12-13)
2. Trick. He had no sleep (Daniel 6:18)
3. an angel (Daniel 6:22)
4. they would be thrown into the lions' den (Daniel 6:24)
5. believed (Daniel 6:23)

Quiz 187: **Daniel's First Recorded Dream**

1. four (Daniel 7:3)
2. four (Daniel 7:6)
3. Trick. It carried three ribs (Daniel 7:5)
4. iron (Daniel 7:7)
5. Ancient (Daniel 7:9)

Quiz 188: **Queen Vashti**

1. Shushan (Esther 1:2)
2. to come to the feast with the royal crown (Esther 1:10-11)
3. fair (Esther 1:11)
4. Trick. She refused completely (Esther 1:12)
5. all the wives of the kingdom (Esther 1:18, 20)

Quiz 189: **Queen Esther**
1. Hadassah (Esther 2:7)
2. his "uncle's daughter," or cousin (Esther 2:7)
3. reveal that she was Jewish (Esther 2:10)
4. Trick. She waited ten months (Esther 2:16)
5. grace (Esther 2:17)

Quiz 190: **Mordecai**
1. in the king's gate (Esther 2:21)
2. Trick. Only two people plotted to kill the king (Esther 2:21)
3. they were hanged (Esther 2:23)
4. in the book of the chronicles (Esther 2:23)
5. told (Esther 2:22)

Quiz 191: **Haman**
1. because Mordecai, who was Jewish, refused to bow or show reverence to Haman (Esther 3:5-6)
2. by casting Pur, or lots (Esther 3:7)
3. True (Esther 4:10-12)
4. because Mordecai had saved the king's life (Esther 6:1-12)
5. time (Esther 4:14)

Quiz 192: **Purim**
1. two (Esther 5:6, 7:2-4)
2. True (Esther 7:10)
3. by writing another law saying they could arm themselves and kill their attackers (Esther 8:11-12)
4. by celebrating Purim every year (Esther 9:21-22, 26)
5. Mordecai (Esther 10:3)

Quiz 193: **Nehemiah**

1. the king of Persia's cupbearer (Nehemiah 1:11)
2. Shushan (Nehemiah 1:1)
3. True (Nehemiah 1:3–4)
4. fasted (Nehemiah 1:4)
5. attentive (Nehemiah 1:6)

Quiz 194: **Nehemiah and the King**

1. sadness (Nehemiah 2:2)
2. pray (Nehemiah 2:4)
3. Trick. Nehemiah requested that the king send him to personally oversee the repairs (Nehemiah 2:5)
4. to obtain timber for construction (Nehemiah 2:8)
5. hand (Nehemiah 2:8)

Quiz 195: **Nehemiah in Jerusalem**

1. three (Nehemiah 2:11)
2. at night (Nehemiah 2:12)
3. Trick. He told no one (Nehemiah 2:12, 16)
4. the king's pool (Nehemiah 2:14)
5. build (Nehemiah 2:18)

Quiz 196: **Nehemiah and the Troublemakers**

1. Sanballat, Tobiah, Geshem (Nehemiah 2:19)
2. True (Nehemiah 4:17)
3. an open letter (Nehemiah 6:5)
4. fifty-two days (Nehemiah 6:15)
5. wrought (Nehemiah 6:16)

Quiz 197: **Rebuilding the Temple**

1. Cyrus (Ezra 1:1–3)
2. True (Ezra 4:1–2)
3. Zerubbabel, Jeshua (Ezra 4:3)
4. Darius (Ezra 4:5)
5. weakened (Ezra 4:4)

Quiz 198: **Temple Delays**

1. rebel and refuse to pay taxes (Ezra 4:12–16)
2. Artaxerxes (Ezra 4:7)
3. Trick. He ordered them to cease (Ezra 4:23)
4. a roll with a written record from Cyrus (Ezra 6:2–3)
5. governor (Ezra 6:13)

Quiz 199: **Finishing the Temple**

1. Haggai, Zechariah (Ezra 5:1)
2. dwelling in nice houses for themselves (Haggai 1:4)
3. True (Haggai 1:6)
4. they listened and obeyed (Haggai 1:12)
5. wood (Haggai 1:8)

Quiz 200: **Ezra Prepares to Return**

1. a fast (Ezra 8:21)
2. soldiers to protect them (Ezra 8:22)
3. True (Ezra 8:22)
4. vessels from Solomon's temple (Ezra 8:30)
5. delivered (Ezra 8:31)

Quiz 201: **End of the Old Testament**
1. "the burden" (Malachi 1:1)
2. they were offering blind, lame, and sick animals (Malachi 1:8)
3. the priests (Malachi 2:7-8)
4. True (Malachi 2:17)
5. Sun (Malachi 4:2)

Quiz 202: **Mary's Angelic Visitor**
1. six months (Luke 1:24-26)
2. Gabriel (Luke 1:26)
3. Trick. Although she was confused, she willingly accepted God's plan (Luke 1:34-38)
4. departed immediately (Luke 1:38)
5. nothing (Luke 1:37)

Quiz 203: **Joseph's Fiancée**
1. True (Matthew 1:18)
2. put her away privily (Matthew 1:19)
3. in a dream (Matthew 1:20)
4. God with us (Matthew 1:23)
5. firstborn (Matthew 1:25)

Quiz 204: **Mary and Elisabeth**
1. to a city of Juda in the hill country (Luke 1:39)
2. her baby leaped within her womb, and she was filled with the Holy Ghost (Luke 1:41)
3. True (Luke 1:59-60)
4. by writing on a tablet (Luke 1:63)
5. believed (Luke 1:45)

Quiz 205: **The First Christmas**
1. Caesar Augustus (Luke 2:1)
2. David's (Luke 2:4)
3. Trick. There was no room for them in the inn (Luke 2:7)
4. a manger (Luke 2:7)
5. city (Luke 2:3)

Quiz 206: **Shepherds Near Bethlehem**
1. nighttime (Luke 2:8)
2. one (Luke 2:9-10)
3. True (Luke 2:15)
4. glorified and praised God, telling everyone what they'd witnessed (Luke 2:17, 20)
5. peace (Luke 2:14)

Quiz 207: **Baby Jesus at the Temple**
1. True (Luke 2:22-23)
2. took him up in his arms and blessed God (Luke 2:25-28)
3. Anna (Luke 2:36-38)
4. she marveled (Luke 2:33)
5. salvation (Luke 2:30)

Quiz 208: **Wise Men**
1. the east (Matthew 2:1)
2. a star (Matthew 2:9)
3. treasures (Matthew 2:11)
4. Trick. Herod was troubled (Matthew 2:3)
5. slew them (Matthew 2:16)

Quiz 209: **Refugees**

1. Jeremiah (Matthew 2:17–18)
2. Egypt (Matthew 2:13)
3. Herod's (Matthew 2:19–20)
4. Trick. They stayed in Galilee (Matthew 2:22)
5. Nazareth (Matthew 2:23)

Quiz 210: **Young Jesus at the Temple**

1. Passover (Luke 2:41)
2. twelve years old (Luke 2:42)
3. a day's journey (Luke 2:44)
4. Trick. All who heard Jesus were astonished at His understanding (Luke 2:47)
5. Father's (Luke 2:49)

Quiz 211: **Jesus' Baptism**

1. John (Matthew 3:14–15)
2. True (Matthew 3:14)
3. thirty years old (Luke 3:23)
4. a dove (Luke 3:22)
5. voice (Mark 1:11)

Quiz 212: **Jesus' Temptations**

1. forty (Mark 1:13)
2. by quoting scripture (Luke 4:4, 8, 10–12)
3. True (Matthew 4:6)
4. the Spirit (Matthew 4:1)
5. tempt (Luke 4:12)

Quiz 213: **Water into Wine**
1. a wedding (John 2:1, 11)
2. Jesus' mother, Mary (John 2:3)
3. do (John 2:5)
4. six (John 2:6, 9)
5. Trick. Only the servants who drew the water knew (John 2:9)

Quiz 214: **The Beatitudes**
1. the meek (Matthew 5:5)
2. poor (Matthew 5:3)
3. those who mourn (Matthew 5:4)
4. Trick. It's the *pure* in heart (Matthew 5:8)
5. they will be filled (Matthew 5:6)

Quiz 215: **Requests in the Lord's Prayer**
1. God's will (Matthew 6:10)
2. bread (Matthew 6:11)
3. Trick. We ask for forgiveness *as* we forgive others (Matthew 6:12)
4. temptation (Matthew 6:13)
5. evil (Matthew 6:13)

Quiz 216: **Matthew**
1. Levi (Mark 2:14; Matthew 9:9)
2. publican (or tax collector) (Luke 5:27)
3. Trick. He followed immediately (Matthew 9:9)
4. the scribes and Pharisees (Luke 5:30)
5. sinners (Luke 5:32)

Quiz 217: **Paralytic on the Roof**

1. four (Mark 2:3)
2. they broke through the roof and lowered the mat to Him (Mark 2:4–5)
3. faith (Mark 2:5)
4. Trick. They never said a word but thought these things in their hearts (Mark 2:6–7)
5. to show that He had the power to forgive sins (Mark 2:8–12)

Quiz 218: **A Woman with a Lengthy Illness**

1. twelve (Luke 8:43)
2. True (Luke 8:43)
3. the border of His garment (Luke 8:44)
4. "Who touched me?" (Luke 8:45)
5. trembling (Luke 8:47)

Quiz 219: **Stampeding Pigs**

1. Legion (Mark 5:9)
2. among the tombs (Mark 5:2–3)
3. Trick. They asked and received Jesus' permission to enter the pigs (Mark 5:12–13)
4. about two thousand (Mark 5:13)
5. home (Mark 5:19)

Quiz 220: **Walking on Water**

1. praying (Mark 6:46–47)
2. True (Mark 6:48)
3. a spirit (Matthew 14:26)
4. Peter (Matthew 14:28–29)
5. worshipped (Matthew 14:33)

Quiz 221: **Feeding the Five Thousand**
1. to prove, or test, him (John 6:6)
2. Andrew (John 6:8-9)
3. twelve (Matthew 14:20)
4. True (Matthew 14:13-21; Mark 6:30-44; Luke 9:10-17; John 6:1-15)
5. Gather (John 6:12)

Quiz 222: **A Nighttime Interview**
1. Nicodemus (John 3:1-2)
2. believeth (John 3:16)
3. be born again (John 3:3)
4. Moses lifting up the serpent in the wilderness (John 3:14)
5. True (John 3:1)

Quiz 223: **Woman at the Well**
1. Samaria (John 4:4-7)
2. Trick. Jesus asked her for water (John 4:7)
3. in the city purchasing food (John 4:8)
4. Christ (John 4:29)
5. two days (John 4:40)

Quiz 224: **Healing a Boy**
1. "a certain nobleman" (John 4:46)
2. True (John 4:47)
3. He spoke the word from another town, Cana (John 4:50)
4. "it was at the same hour" (John 4:53)
5. believe (John 4:48)

Quiz 225: **Healing a Sick Man at Bethesda**

1. True (John 5:3–4)
2. thirty-eight (John 5:5)
3. the Sabbath (John 5:9)
4. twice (John 5:13–15)
5. sin (John 5:14)

Quiz 226: **Some of Jesus' "I AM" Statements**

1. the bread of life (John 6:35)
2. the light of the world (John 8:12)
3. True (John 10:7, 11)
4. the resurrection and the life (John 11:25)
5. truth (John 14:6)

Quiz 227: **The Transfiguration**

1. three (Luke 9:28)
2. Moses, Elijah (Matthew 17:3)
3. white as snow (Mark 9:3)
4. hear (Mark 9:7)
5. True (Matthew 17:9)

Quiz 228: **Mary and Martha**

1. Martha (Luke 10:38)
2. Mary (Luke 10:39)
3. True (Luke 10:40)
4. serve everyone (Luke 10:40)
5. needful (Luke 10:42)

Quiz 229: **Rich Young Ruler**
1. "What shall I do that I may inherit eternal life?" (Mark 10:17)
2. God (Mark 10:18)
3. sell everything, give it to the poor, and follow Him (Luke 18:21)
4. Trick. He went away sorrowful, because of his wealth (Matthew 19:22)
5. impossible (Matthew 19:26)

Quiz 230: **Tax Advice**
1. the Herodians (Mark 12:13)
2. lawful (Mark 12:14)
3. a penny, or denarius (Mark 12:15)
4. Caesar's (Mark 12:16)
5. True (Mark 12:17)

Quiz 231: **The Widow's Offering**
1. near the temple treasury (Mark 12:41)
2. two (John 12:42)
3. Trick. They gave much (Mark 12:41)
4. abundance (Mark 12:44)
5. His disciples (Mark 12:43)

Quiz 232: **Parable of the Wheat and Tares**
1. while men slept (Matthew 13:25)
2. because they'd uproot the wheat too (Matthew 13:29)
3. the world (Matthew 13:38)
4. True (Matthew 13:39)
5. righteous (Matthew 13:43)

Quiz 233: **Parable of the Net**
1. the kingdom of heaven (Matthew 13:47)
2. when it was full (Matthew 13:48)
3. the angels (Matthew 13:49)
4. Trick. It was cast into the sea (Matthew 13:47)
5. furnace (Matthew 13:50)

Quiz 234: **Parable of the Sower**
1. four (Luke 8:5-8)
2. the Word of God (Luke 8:11)
3. keep (Luke 8:15)
4. Trick. Birds ate it (Luke 8:5)
5. choked them (Luke 8:7)

Quiz 235: **Parable of the Good Samaritan**
1. Jericho (Luke 10:30)
2. a priest, a Levite (Luke 10:31-32)
3. Trick. The Samaritan addressed the man's wounds, but took him to an inn and paid the bill (Luke 10:34-35)
4. to repay whatever the host spent while caring for the injured man (Luke 10:35)
5. likewise (Luke 10:37)

Quiz 236: **Parable of the Vineyard Owner**
1. winepress, tower (Matthew 21:33)
2. in a far country (Matthew 21:33)
3. True (Matthew 21:35-36)
4. his son (Matthew 21:37)
5. taken (Matthew 21:43)

Quiz 237: **Parable of the Virgins**

1. the bridegroom (Matthew 25:1)
2. five (Matthew 25:2)
3. midnight (Matthew 25:6)
4. Trick. They were shut out forever (Matthew 25:10–12)
5. not (Matthew 25:12)

Quiz 238: **Parable of the Talents**

1. five (Matthew 25:15)
2. True (Matthew 25:18)
3. two more (Matthew 25:22)
4. the third servant, who had one talent (Matthew 25:25–28)
5. away (Matthew 25:29)

Quiz 239: **Parable of the Wedding Banquet**

1. the kingdom of heaven (Matthew 22:2)
2. none (Matthew 22:3)
3. True (Matthew 22:10)
4. he was bound hand and foot, taken away, and cast into outer darkness (Matthew 22:13)
5. chosen (Matthew 22:14)

Quiz 240: **Parable of the Lost Sheep**

1. ninety-nine (Luke 15:4)
2. Trick. He simply rejoiced (Luke 15:5)
3. on his shoulders (Luke 15:5)
4. called together his friends and neighbors (Luke 15:6)
5. Rejoice (Luke 15:6)

Quiz 241: **Parable of the Lost Coin**

1. nine (Luke 15:8)
2. silver (Luke 15:8)
3. True (Luke 15:8)
4. called her friends and neighbors together (Luke 15:9)
5. joy (Luke 15:10)

Quiz 242: **A Woman Who Couldn't Straighten Up**

1. eighteen (Luke 13:11)
2. the Sabbath (Luke 13:14)
3. Trick. He was angry that she was healed on the Sabbath (Luke 13:14)
4. care for their animals (Luke 13:15)
5. rejoiced (Luke 13:17)

Quiz 243: **Jesus Heals Lepers**

1. ten (Luke 17:15-17)
2. True (Luke 17:14-15)
3. nine (Luke 17:15)
4. Samaritan (Luke 17:16)
5. faith (Luke 17:19)

Quiz 244: **Blind Bartimaeus**

1. they told him to be quiet (Mark 10:47-48)
2. He stood still and sent for Bartimaeus (Mark 10:49)
3. Jericho (Luke 10:46)
4. Trick. Jesus healed Bartimaeus immediately because the man had faith (Mark 10:52)
5. praise (Luke 18:43)

Quiz 245: **Zacchaeus**

1. He was short and couldn't see Jesus because of the crowd (Luke 19:3)
2. sycomore (Luke 19:4)
3. True (Luke 19:5)
4. joyfully (Luke 19:6)
5. salvation (Luke 19:9)

Quiz 246: **The Anointing at Bethany**

1. a pound (John 12:3)
2. her hair (John 12:3)
3. Judas Iscariot (Matthew 26:8; John 12:4–5)
4. True (John 12:6)
5. burying (John 12:7)

Quiz 247: **Palm Sunday**

1. two (Mark 11:1–2)
2. two (Matthew 21:2)
3. Trick. They were to say, "Because the Lord hath need of him" (Luke 19:31)
4. for a feast, Passover (John 12:12)
5. stones (Luke 19:40)

Quiz 248: **Foot Washing**

1. a towel, water in a basin (John 13:4–5)
2. Peter (John 13:8)
3. True (John 13:2, 11–12)
4. to give them an example of what they should do for others (John 13:15)
5. servant (John 13:16)

Quiz 249: **A Plot to Kill Jesus**

1. Lazarus, whom Jesus had raised from the dead (John 12:10–11)
2. thirty (Matthew 27:3)
3. hanged (Matthew 27:5)
4. Trick. They bought a potter's field (Matthew 27:5-7)
5. Caiaphas, the high priest (John 11:49–50)

Quiz 250: **Peter Denies Jesus**

1. True (John 18:15–16)
2. three (Luke 22:61)
3. a cock, or rooster (Matthew 26:75)
4. twice (Mark 14:72)
5. bitterly (Luke 22:62)

Quiz 251: **Jesus vs. the Sanhedrin**

1. True (Matthew 26:59–60)
2. it didn't agree (Mark 14:56)
3. striking His face (Luke 22:64)
4. Annas, Caiaphas' father-in-law (John 18:13)
5. guilty (Matthew 26:66)

Quiz 252: **Jesus Arrested**

1. he kissed Jesus (Matthew 26:47–48)
2. they went backward and fell to the ground (John 18:5–6)
3. True (Mark 14:51–52)
4. Malchus (John 18:10)
5. fulfilled (Matthew 26:54)

Quiz 253: **Jesus before Herod**
1. Pilate (Luke 23:6–7)
2. True (Luke 23:8)
3. He didn't—He said nothing (Luke 23:9)
4. Pilate (Luke 23:12)
5. glad (Luke 23:8)

Quiz 254: **Jesus or Barabbas**
1. insurrection, murder, robbery (Mark 15:7; John 18:40)
2. Trick. It was Pilate's wife who warned him (Matthew 27:19)
3. a troubling dream (Matthew 27:19)
4. the chief priests and elders (Matthew 27:20)
5. content (Mark 15:15)

Quiz 255: **Soldiers Mock Jesus**
1. purple (Mark 15:17)
2. thorns (John 19:2)
3. a reed (Matthew 27:29)
4. True (Matthew 27:29–30)
5. crucify (Matthew 27:31)

Quiz 256: **Crucified**
1. Cyrene (Mark 15:21)
2. Calvary (Luke 23:33)
3. myrrh (Mark 15:23)
4. Trick. The soldiers cast lots for the clothes (Mark 15:24)
5. accusation (Mark 15:26)

Quiz 257: **Two Criminals**

1. True (Matthew 27:44)
2. to save Himself and them (Luke 23:39)
3. he rebuked him (Luke 23:40)
4. to remember him when Jesus came into His kingdom (Luke 23:42)
5. paradise (Luke 23:43)

Quiz 258: **Jesus' Death**

1. "My God, my God, why hast thou forsaken me?" (Matthew 27:46)
2. it was torn in two from top to bottom (Matthew 27:51)
3. True (Matthew 27:52-53)
4. the Son of God (Matthew 27:54)
5. finished (John 19:30)

Quiz 259: **Jesus' Burial**

1. Pilate (Mark 15:44)
2. blood, water (John 19:34)
3. Joseph of Arimathaea, Nicodemus (John 19:38-39)
4. Trick. Jesus was buried in a tomb in which no one had been buried (Luke 23:53)
5. stone (Matthew 27:60)

Quiz 260: **Jesus' Resurrection**

1. early, when it was yet dark (Matthew 28:1; John 20:1)
2. True (Matthew 28:2)
3. the other disciple, whom Jesus loved (John 20:2)
4. Jesus' dead body (Matthew 28:6)
5. living (Luke 24:5-6)

Quiz 261: **Soldiers Guarding the Tomb**

1. the chief priests, Pharisees (Matthew 27:62-64)
2. True (Matthew 27:63-64)
3. chief priests (Matthew 28:11)
4. a large sum of money and protection from the governor (Matthew 28:12-14)
5. saying (Matthew 28:15)

Quiz 262: **Jesus Appears to Mary Magdalene**

1. she ran to tell Peter and another disciple (John 20:1-2)
2. weeping (John 20:11)
3. Trick. She thought He was a gardener (John 20:15)
4. touch Him (John 20:17)
5. Master (John 20:16)

Quiz 263: **Doubting Thomas**

1. he wasn't present the first time Jesus appeared to the disciples (John 20:24)
2. put his finger into Jesus' nail prints, thrust his hand into Jesus' side (John 20:25)
3. Trick. He had to wait eight days (John 20:26)
4. "My Lord and my God" (John 20:28)
5. blessed (John 20:29)

Quiz 264: **On the Road to Emmaus**

1. two (Luke 24:13)
2. True (Luke 24:15-16)
3. the events of the past week, including the empty tomb (Luke 24:17-24)
4. broke bread and gave it to them (Luke 24:30-31)
5. heart (Luke 24:32)

Quiz 265: **Jesus Serves Breakfast**
1. the Sea of Tiberias, or Galilee (John 21:1)
2. Trick. They caught nothing (John 21:3)
3. the right side (John 21:6)
4. 153 (John 21:11)
5. fish and bread (John 21:9)

Quiz 266: **Peter Restored**
1. because he had jumped into the sea to get to Jesus on shore (John 21:7–8)
2. Trick. Jesus asked three times (John 21:17)
3. feed them (John 21:15–17)
4. True (John 21:18–19)
5. Follow (John 21:19)

Quiz 267: **The Ascension**
1. leave Jerusalem (Acts 1:4)
2. a cloud (Acts 1:9)
3. two men in white apparel (Acts 1:10)
4. witnesses (Acts 1:8)
5. True (Acts 1:6–7)

Quiz 268: **Pentecost**
1. a rushing mighty wind (Acts 2:2)
2. cloven tongues of fire (Acts 2:3)
3. they could speak in many tongues and languages (Acts 2:4, 6–11)
4. True (Acts 2:13)
5. Galilaeans (Acts 2:7)

Quiz 269: **The Fatal Lie**

1. husband and wife (Acts 5:1)
2. that they'd given all the proceeds from a land sale to the church (Acts 5:3, 8)
3. True (Acts 5:3–5, 8–10)
4. Peter (Acts 5:3, 8)
5. conceived (Acts 5:4)

Quiz 270: **Prison Break**

1. the apostles (Acts 5:16–18)
2. the angel of the Lord (Acts 5:19)
3. back at the temple, preaching the gospel (Acts 5:25)
4. Trick. It was Gamaliel (Acts 5:34–39)
5. obey (Acts 5:29)

Quiz 271: **Stephen**

1. to care for the needs of the Grecian widows (Acts 6:1–5)
2. great wonders and miracles (Acts 6:8)
3. his spirit and undisputable wisdom (Acts 6:10)
4. True (Acts 7:58, 13:9)
5. full (Acts 7:55)

Quiz 272: **An Ethiopian Official's Conversion**

1. the angel of the Lord (Acts 8:26)
2. Philip (Acts 8:26)
3. sitting in his chariot (Acts 8:27–28)
4. Trick. He was reading from the prophet Isaiah (Acts 8:30)
5. believe (Acts 8:37)

Quiz 273: **Saul's Dramatic Conversion**

1. Damascus (Acts 9:2)
2. Trick. The men heard the voice but saw no man (Acts 9:7)
3. three (Acts 9:9)
4. Ananias (Acts 9:10–18)
5. chosen (Acts 9:15)

Quiz 274: **Saul's Escape over the Wall**

1. the gates of Damascus (Acts 9:24)
2. the disciples (Acts 9:25)
3. a basket (Acts 9:25)
4. True (Acts 9:27)
5. boldly (Acts 9:29)

Quiz 275: **Dorcas**

1. Tabitha (Acts 9:36)
2. coats and garments (Acts 9:39)
3. Peter (Acts 9:40)
4. Trick. It happened near Joppa (Acts 9:36–38)
5. alive (Acts 9:41)

Quiz 276: **Peter and Cornelius**

1. centurion (Acts 10:1)
2. an angel of God (Acts 10:3)
3. True (Acts 10:11–14)
4. three (Acts 10:16)
5. unclean (Acts 10:28)

Quiz 277: **Apostolic Prison Break**

1. Trick. It was Peter (Acts 12:6)
2. shine a light, hit him on the side, and tell him, "Arise up quickly" (Acts 12:7)
3. he was having a vision (Acts 12:9)
4. Rhoda (Acts 12:14)
5. angel (Acts 12:15)

Quiz 278: **Herod's Painful Death**

1. making an oration (Acts 12:21)
2. True (Acts 12:22)
3. for not giving God the glory (Acts 12:23)
4. he was smitten by an angel and eaten by worms (Acts 12:23)
5. multiplied (Acts 12:24)

Quiz 279: **Mission Field Preparations**

1. Antioch (Acts 13:1–3)
2. five (Acts 13:1)
3. Barnabas, Saul (Acts 13:2)
4. Trick. They fasted and prayed (Acts 13:3)
5. Cyprus (Acts 13:4)

Quiz 280: **Mistaken for Gods**

1. Lystra (Acts 14:18)
2. Paul and Barnabas healed a man crippled since birth (Acts 14:8–11)
3. True (Acts 14:12)
4. rent, or tore, them (Acts 14:14)
5. passions (Acts 14:15)

Quiz 281: **Missionary Squabble**

1. John Mark (Acts 15:37)
2. he left the other at Pamphylia instead of working with them (Acts 15:38)
3. True (Acts 15:39)
4. he sailed to Cyprus with Barnabas (Acts 15:39)
5. Silas (Acts 15:40)

Quiz 282: **Timothy Enters the Picture**

1. Paul (Acts 16:3)
2. Trick. The opposite was true (Acts 16:1)
3. Lystra, Iconium (Acts 16:2)
4. so as to not upset the Jews (Acts 16:3)
5. churches (Acts 16:5)

Quiz 283: **Lydia**

1. Trick. She was from Thyatira, but Paul met her in Philippi (Acts 16:12-14)
2. a seller of purple (Acts 16:14)
3. by a river side (Acts 16:13)
4. stay at her home while they did missionary work in the area (Acts 16:15)
5. heart (Acts 16:14)

Quiz 284: **Fortune-Telling Slave Girl**

1. True (Acts 16:17)
2. commanded the spirit to leave the girl (Acts 16:18-19)
3. ordered them beaten and thrown into prison (Acts 16:20-23)
4. put their feet in stocks in the inner prison (Acts 16:24)
5. Jews (Acts 16:20)

Quiz 285: **Yet Another Jail Break**

1. prayed, sang praises to God (Acts 16:25)
2. an earthquake (Acts 16:26)
3. Trick. No one left, even though they could have (Acts 16:28)
4. he became a believer in Jesus (Acts 16:27–34)
5. saved (Acts 16:31)

Quiz 286: **Corinthian Church Start-Up**

1. the Corinthian Jews' repeated opposition and blasphemy (Acts 18:4–6)
2. tentmaker (Acts 18:3)
3. True (Acts 18:8)
4. a year and six months (Acts 18:11)
5. afraid (Acts 18:9)

Quiz 287: **Riot in Ephesus**

1. Demetrius (Acts 19:24)
2. True (Acts 19:24–27)
3. Diana (Acts 19:27)
4. two hours (Acts 19:34–35)
5. rashly (Acts 19:36)

Quiz 288: **Eutychus' Miracle**

1. in a third-story window (Acts 20:9)
2. midnight (Acts 20:7)
3. True (Acts 20:9)
4. Paul (Acts 20:10–11)
5. alive (Acts 20:12)

Quiz 289: **A Plot to Kill**

1. Trick. They plotted to kill Paul (Acts 23:12)
2. more than forty (Acts 23:13)
3. Paul's nephew (Acts 23:16)
4. the chief captain (Acts 23:17)
5. Caesarea (Acts 23:23)

Quiz 290: **Paul Shipped to Rome**

1. True (Acts 27:9–10)
2. three (Acts 27:19)
3. fourteen (Acts 27:27)
4. the shipmen (Acts 27:30)
5. meat (Acts 27:34)

Quiz 291: **Shipwreck!**

1. it was broken apart by the violent waves (Acts 27:41)
2. kill them so they couldn't escape (Acts 27:42)
3. the centurion (Acts 27:43)
4. True (Acts 27:44)
5. safe (Acts 27:44)

Quiz 292: **Island Hospitality**

1. Trick. It was cold and raining (Acts 28:2)
2. a viper (Acts 28:3)
3. murder (Acts 28:4)
4. a god (Acts 28:6)
5. Melita (Acts 28:1)

Quiz 293: **Island Miracle**
1. Publius, chief man of the island (Acts 28:7–8)
2. hands (Acts 28:8)
3. Trick. Many came to him for healing of their diseases (Acts 28:9)
4. three months (Acts 28:11)
5. Castor and Pollux (Acts 28:11)

Quiz 294: **Love, or Charity**
1. nothing (1 Corinthians 13:2)
2. the truth (1 Corinthians 13:6)
3. Trick. Love is the greatest (1 Corinthians 13:13)
4. beareth, believeth, hopeth, endureth (1 Corinthians 13:7)
5. fail (1 Corinthians 13:8)

Quiz 295: **The Whole Armour of God**
1. flesh and blood (Ephesians 6:12)
2. Trick. Righteousness is represented by a breastplate—the helmet is salvation (Ephesians 6:14, 17)
3. the fiery darts of the wicked (Ephesians 6:16)
4. praying (Ephesians 6:18)
5. stand (Ephesians 6:13)

Quiz 296: **Philemon**
1. Trick. The opposite was true (verses 10–16)
2. he was aged (verse 9)
3. nothing—he merely asked him to lovingly take Onesimus in again (verses 8–9, 14)
4. to pay back anything the one-time slave owed (verses 18–19)
5. unprofitable (verse 11)

Quiz 297: **Letters to Seven Churches**
1. its candlestick (Revelation 2:5)
2. Laodicea (Revelation 3:14–16)
3. Spirit (Revelation 2:29)
4. Philadelphia (Revelation 3:7–8)
5. True (Revelation 2:17)

Quiz 298: **End Times**
1. Trick: The reverse order is true—seven seals, seven trumpets, seven bowls (Revelation 6:1, 8:6, 16:1)
2. one thousand (Revelation 20:1–3)
3. witnesses (Revelation 11:3)
4. anyone not found written in the book of life (Revelation 20:15)
5. God Himself (Revelation 21:3)

Quiz 299: **The Great White Throne of Judgment**
1. the earth, the heaven (Revelation 20:11)
2. True (Revelation 20:12)
3. the small and the great (Revelation 20:12)
4. their works (Revelation 20:13)
5. whosoever (Revelation 20:15)

Quiz 300: **New Jerusalem**
1. True (Revelation 21:1)
2. from God out of heaven (Revelation 21:2)
3. twelve (Revelation 21:12)
4. precious stones (Revelation 21:19)
5. tabernacle (Revelation 21:3)

Love Bible Trivia?

365 DAYS OF BIBLE TRIVIA

QUESTIONS & ANSWERS
for Morning & Evening

Here are two questions a day for an entire year to test your memory and enhance your knowledge of God's Word. What do you remember of the people, places, things, and ideas of the Old and New Testaments? Put on your thinking cap and find out here!

Paperback / ISBN 978-1-63609-498-4

Find This and More from Barbour Publishing at Your Favorite Bookstore or www.barbourbooks.com

BARBOUR
PUBLISHING